"Masters of procrastination, ALERT! To end your procrastination, read this book."
– Mark Victor Hansen, coauthor of the
Chicken Soup for the Soul series

"Since I read this marvelously helpful, entertaining book, the piles of work on my desk have dramatically decreased. We can now see the window! What a pleasure to follow these rules, then—wham! bang!—one job is complete and I pick up the next, knowing I can finish it today."
– Dottie Walters, author of *Speak & Grow Rich*
and president of Walters International Speakers Bureau

"This great little book shows you how to eliminate procrastination once and for all—the *key* to peak performance and maximum productivity!"
– Brian Tracy, Brian Tracy International

"Besides having an outrageous sense of humor and fun, Rita Emmett is, above all, down-to-earth and practical. This book will inspire you, delight you, challenge you, and guide you."
– Barbara Glanz, author of *CARE Packages for the Workplace* and *Care Packages for the Home*

"This is the best book I've read on procrastination. This isn't written for psychologists, it's written for you and me. You're going to love it."
– Hal Roach, author of *We Irish Talk Like That* and *Write It Down*

The
PROCRASTINATOR'S
HANDBOOK

To Lucy

Rita Emmett

THE

Procrastinator's Handbook

MASTERING THE ART OF DOING IT NOW

Rita Emmett

Walker & Company
New York

To protect the privacy of seminar participants who have given
permission for their stories to appear in this book, their names
and identifying characteristics have been changed.

First published in the United States of America in 2000 by
Walker Publishing Company, Inc.

Library of Congress Cataloging-in-Publication Data
Emmett, Rita.
    The procrastinator's handbook : mastering the art of doing
    it now / Rita Emmett.
        p. cm.
    ISBN 0-8027-1356-4—ISBN 0-8027-7598-5 (pbk.)
    1. Procrastination. I. Title.

BF637.P76E48 2000
155.2'32—dc21

                                            00-034954

Book design by Dede Cummings
Illustrations on pages 19, 38, 99, 117, 154, and 203 by Carol Stephens

Printed in Canada

2 4 6 8 10 9 7 5 3 1

To my husband, best friend, and favorite traveling companion, Bruce Karder, and to the shining delights of our lives, our blended family of five kids and four kids-in-law who give us so much joy in so many ways, including blessing us with seven glorious grandchildren (who are also smart, talented, gorgeous, and more, but I don't want to brag). Thank you, God.

Contents

Acknowledgments

๛

MANY PEOPLE HELPED and encouraged me in bringing this book to its present state, and I am so grateful to all of them. If I have omitted anyone, I apologize for my absentmindedness. The memory is the second thing to go.... I don't remember what the first thing is.

I want to thank and acknowledge Julie Hurlbut, who was there from the start, as well as Robb Emmett, Ruth Coleman, Georgia Impastato, Patty Dorney, Jack Finney, and Pat Connelley.

It's not easy to get people to read *and* critique a book in progress. Thanks from the bottom of my heart to my cherished niece Mickey Forster and good friend Kathy Hartwig, who were there from start to finish, and to the other magnificent readers, Michelle Emmett, Tom Dorney, Curt Hansen, Julie Seely, Cec Hanec, Stephen McShane, Tiffany Marshall, and Joanna Slan.

When computers threatened to drive me insane, four wonderful computer gurus came to my rescue. Thank you

Mickey Forster (who seemed to bail me out of trouble at least once every week), Dolores Kalayta, Kym Karder, and Bill Metcalf.

I'm eternally grateful to the two Loretto sisters, who taught me about writing; to my high school English teachers Maria Bierer, IBVM, and Jeannette Shean, IBVM; and for all the coaching I received from Barb Glanz, Dottie Walters, Joel Roberts, Mark Victor Hansen, Robert Jackway, and Dan Poynter.

Heartfelt appreciation to my agent, Jane Jordan Browne, who once upon a time terrified me and still continues to make up rules about when I'm allowed to disagree with her, and to my editor, Jackie Johnson, who polished away the rough edges with a smile and through gritted teeth allowed me to keep the Yoda quotation.

And finally, the best support in the world came from my husband, Bruce. He hasn't read one word of this book—and possibly never will—but the man grocery shops and does laundry. Who could ask for anything more? (I have *my* priorities straight.)

Thank you and God bless you all.

The
PROCRASTINATOR'S
HANDBOOK

Introduction

꿎

DO YOU PUT OFF DOING things that are really important to you? Do you sometimes feel anxious or guilty because you just can't get yourself to do what you need or want to do? Is your procrastination driving your family, friends, and/or coworkers crazy?

Procrastination can take a surprisingly high toll on your life, causing stress, illness, and low self-esteem. It keeps you from attaining your goals and fulfilling your dreams. If you're a procrastinator, you might answer yes to one or more of the following questions:

- Do you pay fees for bounced checks, late payments of bills, or high-interest credit card balances because you put off routine personal finance chores? As a result, are you paying so much money to "catch up" that you can never get ahead?

- Do you want to start an exercise program, or begin other healthy habits, or set up an appointment with your doctor or dentist, but you never do?

- Are you losing the battle against clutter on your desk, dining room table, counters, closets, or floors? Does the chaos in the space around you seem to create chaos in your mind and your spirit, leaving you feeling overwhelmed, out of control, and exhausted?

Well, there *is* hope. In this book about the frustrating, fascinating, and—yes—funny subject of procrastination, I will show you how to stop putting off things, become more productive, and develop priorities that reflect your personal goals and values.

As a professional speaker, I give presentations all over the United States, teaching principles and strategies for conquering procrastination. Years ago when I was presenting Time Management seminars, I heard several people saying they didn't sign up for Time Management "because none of that stuff ever works for me." After talking with them, I discovered that they were all procrastinators whose unique needs were not being addressed by time management books and seminars.

People who benefit from time management are like a group that has decided to go on a bicycle journey. They know where they want to go; their bikes are all ready, and time management principles are like the map or directions they need to set off on their adventure.

Then along comes the group of procrastinators meandering down the road. They haven't decided yet where they want to go, and they've forgotten to bring their bikes, which don't work anyway because they haven't gotten around to fixing the flat tire. Maps and directions (time management principles) are of little use to this group. They need something different, so for them I developed my Conquer Procrastination seminars and wrote this book.

When people take my seminars, often the first questions they ask are: "Can a person really stop procrastinating?" "How can people expect to change their basic personalities or character traits?"

Procrastination is not an inherent part of your personality or character; it is simply a habit, an attitude. Can people change habits? Of course they can! Millions of people have stopped smoking, even though that habit is extremely hard to break. Can people change attitudes? Sure. Do you know anyone who used to think owning a VCR or sending E-mail was unnecessary, yet now—several years later—can't imagine living without either?

I speak about procrastination from personal experience because I used to put off everything. This is the book I wish I'd had when I was struggling to conquer my own procrastinating ways, and when I was designing those early seminars. The only "conquer procrastination" books back then were written for psychologists and tended to be quite dry.

For as long as I can remember, I practiced every delaying, guilt-producing procrastination tactic imaginable. When I was a college student many years ago, I married, got a job, and continued college part-time. But after our son, Robby, was born, I decided to interrupt my studies and my career and become a stay-at-home mom. I had only one semester to complete, so I was certain I could finish my degree fairly quickly as soon as he was older. However, being a confirmed procrastinator, I did not take even one class during the seven years I stayed home to raise Robb and his younger sister, Kerry.

Then I was hired for a job that required a college degree. The time to register for my last semester came—and passed. I did nothing . . . except wallow in guilt and make excuses to my boss.

People offered advice. I listened. Still I did nothing.

During this period of my life, I read a time management book, which said that we procrastinate for one of two reasons: because we are overwhelmed, or because the project is unpleasant. But I didn't consider one semester to be overwhelming, and I didn't find college unpleasant. From my own experience, I realized that there are many other reasons we procrastinate, starting with fear.

I was terrified of going back to school. And when I started to explore my fears, I realized I was scared of many things: Failure. Rejection. Looking foolish. Competing with nineteen-year-old students. Discovering my brain had turned to mush and that I was now stupid. Facing my kids if I received an F in a class. Having to find time to do my homework. Neglecting my children to make time for my classes and homework, and becoming a rotten mother.

These fears were a huge, unknown force that had the power to immobilize me until I started to identify them. Then I could sort through them, talk about them, face them, wrestle with them, come up with some answers, and ultimately move on with my life. I began to practice all the principles you'll read about in this book (including a whole chapter on fear).

Did it work? You bet! About a year later, I proudly joined my classmates walking across the stage to receive my bachelor of arts degree. Five years after that, in addition to raising a family and working, I earned a master's degree. Once you begin conquering procrastination, the sky's the limit.

Now I'm a recovering procrastinator and have been for decades. When I first started using the principles in this book, my only expectation was that they would help me stop putting off tasks, errands, chores, and maybe a few goals. But as I began to convert from my old procrastinating ways, over the years I started to make more and more substantial changes in my life. Eventually, my whole life turned around.

Yours can, too.

This book will enable you to:

- understand and modify some of your unproductive ways of thinking
- identify the games you play and behavioral styles you use for putting things off
- apply proven antiprocrastination tips
- develop strategies to move forward when you're stuck or reverting to your old procrastination patterns
- design your own personal action plans

You will recognize yourself in the real-life stories of people who worked through their procrastination tendencies. Each chapter also has quotes to inspire and motivate you. When a particular saying seems tailor-made for you, copy it and put it where you can see it often.

The "Extra Credit" section at the end of each chapter helps you take the information you've read and personalize it by applying the book's principles to your life. If you like answering questions and measuring your progress, this section is for you. If you'd rather skip the exercises, you don't need to do them; but at least look at each exercise. You might find them interesting, perhaps even fun.

Whether you procrastinate all the time, most of the time or only occasionally, this is the right book for you and the right time for you to be reading it. You're on the verge of climbing out of the procrastination pit. Let's get started . . . right now.

PART I

Getting
a Grip on
Procrastination

1

Tackling
the Dread

*Emmett's Law: The dread of doing a task uses up more time
and energy than doing the task itself.*

HOW MUCH TIME, ENERGY, AND emotion have
you spent agonizing or feeling guilty about putting off
something, only to discover that once you finally get
started, the job takes just a short time?

In one of my Conquer Procrastination seminars, a participant named David, who was a sales manager supervising
fifty-eight sales representatives, told the following story: He
had purchased hundreds of dollars' worth of framed wall
prints with motivational quotations to decorate the sales of-
fices in the new corporate headquarters. Five months after
the move, the walls of David's division were still bare, the
framed prints were still in the storage closets, and David
kept putting off hanging them because he didn't have a
whole day to devote to "decorating the office."

He didn't want to entrust the job to the maintenance men or anyone else because he was positive they would not hang the prints in the proper spots and moving them would leave holes in the walls. Finally growing tired of all the comments and complaints about the naked walls, David decided he'd take some time after lunch each day to hang the prints. When he finished, his whole office area looked marvelous, everyone loved the beauty and spirit of the prints, and David was shocked to realize the whole job—which he had put off for almost half a year—had been incredibly easy and had taken only forty-seven minutes to complete.

Dreaders often have absolutely no idea how long it takes to do whatever job they've been dreading. Are you living in chaos because you're putting off a thirteen-minute job? You may be living an extremely busy life, but do you realize it takes less than two minutes to hang up your clothes or toss them in the clothes hamper?

Are you constantly shuffling through piles of paper on your desk? You probably spend more time shuffling each day than it would take you to sort through the papers once and for all—filing, processing, tossing out, or recycling.

You may procrastinate because you don't want to devote a whole weekend to cleaning the basement or garage, or a whole afternoon to writing that marketing letter. You don't get around to doing these things because you think you never have enough time. The first step is to realize that the job probably won't take the entire weekend or afternoon or however much time you think it will.

The next step involves the use of an ordinary kitchen timer. You may not have a whole weekend to spend on a certain task, but you may be able to find one hour. (Of course, some really great procrastinators can take so many "breaks" that a one-hour project is still unfinished three months later.) So set the timer for sixty minutes and devote one *uninterrupted* hour to the project. No coffee breaks. No phone calls. If you don't have voice mail and you must answer the phone, put some urgency in your voice and tell the other party you can't talk now but that you'll call them back later.

One of three things will happen:

1. You'll finish the job and be amazed at how little time it took. In the future, if you start dreading a similar task, remind yourself that "it takes only thirty-two minutes" or however long it actually took.
2. You'll discover it is such an enormous project that it will take many more hours to complete, but you've made a small dent in it. Decide when to spend another hour on this job. Will you set the timer again once a day? Once a week? Will the timetable be sporadic? Now you have a plan, and you've already accomplished something. For today, you are finished and are no longer haunted by the Dread.
3. At the hour's end you're not finished, but you see the light at the end of the tunnel. This is the most likely scenario. Once you've gained momentum, you won't want to stop. You may actually enjoy pushing ahead to complete the project.

Regardless of how much you do in an hour, you will learn one of the most important lessons in conquering procrastination: What you dread most isn't spending time and energy on the whole job, but simply getting started.

THOSE JOBS YOU HATE TO DO

One of the most obvious reasons for procrastinating is often the most overlooked. The job is put off because it is unpleasant: it's an I-Don't-Like-Doing-It job. For example, Terry can never find time to do routine maintenance on his car because it's a hassle; Deb procrastinates with her physical fitness program because exercise is boring; Tomas puts off calling a client about her tax return because he hates giving bad news.

It's a common human trait to put off jobs we do not like to do. But life seems to overflow with miserable, boring, unpleasant tasks, and somehow they must be completed or problems and stress will result. The problems can be short-term or long-term.

Examples of short-term problems are Terry's car breaking down at the most inconvenient time and Tomas's client becoming unhappy because he didn't call her. Examples of long-term problems would be when Terry has to buy a replacement car before he can afford it, and when Tomas loses the disgruntled client (who finds someone else to do her tax return) and thereby loses a source of income.

It is easiest and most common to put off projects that have long-term consequences. Many people believe they can delay forever planning an exercise program—and they do. To them, it seems that the consequences of suffering poor health will never occur—but they do. Eventually, someone pays a price for procrastinating about any unpleasant task.

So what do you do about the miserable, boring jobs you love to put off? Before coming up with a plan of action, we need to wrestle with some attitudes that foster procrastination.

To begin with, nobody, nowhere, has a life filled with pleasantness, totally devoid of unpleasantness. As Scott Peck writes in the opening line of *The Road Less Traveled*, "Life is difficult." If you are seeking the perfect job or lifestyle that will release you forever from having to do unpleasant chores, you won't find it. It does not exist. So accept the fact that if you want to be a functioning human being, you will be stuck doing some miserable, boring tasks.

The day you say to yourself, "I hate doing this but I have to, so I may as well do it now and get it over with," you will free yourself from the guilt and stress caused by putting it off. And once some of the guilt and stress of procrastination are eliminated from your life, you'll find yourself functioning at a higher level and feeling happier and freer than you could imagine.

Furthermore, doing an unpleasant job often results in pleasant consequences, or at least a wonderful feeling of satisfaction once the job is completed. It's a terrific feeling to say that the bills are paid or a difficult phone call has been made or the project is finished. Even if the boss doesn't notice that your proposal was written before the deadline, you know—and you're the one who can bask in the feeling of satisfaction.

It's amazing how many pleasant feelings in life are preceded by unpleasant or boring jobs. Once you change your attitude and resign yourself to doing those miserable tasks, you'll be ready to discover one of the secrets to conquering procrastination (a secret most of us heard as kids): Do the I-Don't-Like-Doing-It job first.

Jan, another participant in one of my Conquer Procrastination seminars, was the founder of a very successful employment agency. During her first year in business, she took my advice to do the "crummy" job first and was astounded at how quickly it became a habit. For Jan, the hated task was making cold calls. She would often let herself become so swamped with paperwork and administrative duties that by the end of the day she hadn't made even one call to a prospective client. Meanwhile, the dread and anxiety and guilt surrounding her procrastination about those calls would haunt her, even after she left work. Sometimes at night as she was falling asleep, she'd be mentally kicking herself for not making those calls.

When I recommended she get them all out of the way first thing in the morning, she was resistant, but finally agreed to try this plan for the next three weeks. She blocked off several hours each morning (marked on her calendar) for cold calling, taped reminder signs around her desk, and stuck to her commitment. By the end of her three-week "trial period," she'd developed the habit of getting her dreaded job out of the way at the start of her day. Now it's just part of her regular routine. She no longer has the dread hanging over her head all day long, causing anxiety and guilt, and she has much greater success in reaching her prospects. She also regularly meets her sales goals, and her agency has become one of the most successful and respected employment agencies in her city.

Initially, it's extremely difficult to force yourself to do the unpleasant tasks first, but in a short time, this can become a habit. And your life becomes easier. Because much of procrastination is a game—a mind game—you can use your mind to change the game. Instead of focusing on how you'll feel doing the work, focus on how you'll feel when it's finished. Think about the payoff. Visualize the relief and sense of accomplishment you will feel once it is done.

Don't tell yourself, "Woe is me, such misery, I hate doing this." Tell yourself, "I'm going to feel marvelous when this is done." Let your imagination run wild. Picture telling your friends about your accomplishments. Visualize newspaper headlines spelling out every step of your achievement. Harness your mind and imagination to change the procrastination game.

How to Make Boring Jobs
More Enjoyable

Are you procrastinating about doing a particular task because it is boring? What can you do to reduce the boredom? Try playing music or listening to the radio while you work. Mickey, an accountant, listens to the radio while she organizes and files papers, and goes through her E-mails. Traci says her children always played their music in the backyard when cleaning the garage, helping in the garden, or doing yard work. She grumbled and told them to turn it down, but now she admits she finds music to be energizing (even their music).

Take the sting out of balancing the checkbook, catching up on correspondence, or cleaning out old files by doing the work while watching TV, during the commercials. Call a friend and visit by phone while you wash the dishes, fold laundry, clean the kitchen, or do other routine chores.

Remember reading about the pioneers' quilting bees and barn-raising parties? See if you can work together with a family member or friend on a boring chore. The time flies when you are doing the work with someone else.

Consider the example of two young homemakers in my neighborhood who get together in each other's kitchens to make jelly and can vegetables from their gardens. They also have started sewing, so they cut the material for outfits together too. They have fun visiting with each other, their kids play together, and by the end of the day, they have accomplished a lot of work. Plus they've helped each other learn some old-fashioned skills.

Another example: The public relations director of a fast-growing speakers' bureau used to hate to assemble promotional packets because the job was boring. Now she and the publicist share the collating, folding, and stuffing of the promo material while brainstorming about publicity campaigns.

WHICH PART OF THE JOB DO YOU HATE?

Sometimes you procrastinate not because you find the whole job unpleasant, but because you hate one aspect of it. If that's the case, tackle that part first. For example, if you dread writing a summary of the board meeting because tracking down the statistics makes you crazy, try to find a more convenient way to assemble the figures you need instead of putting off preparing the whole summary.

If it's difficult for you to keep track of the phone calls you have to make, go to an office supply store and see if there's some product or system that may solve your problem. If your employer won't supply what you need to be organized, buy it for yourself. You deserve it. Your investment in yourself will save you time, frustration, and aggravation in the long run and show your employer you are a problem solver who takes the initiative.

Susan worked at a community college and seemed to be productive in most areas of her work, with the exception of publicity for special events. She would leave everything till the last minute, and as a result, the public wouldn't hear about the event in time and attendance would be low. As Susan analyzed the problem, it occurred to her that she couldn't stand the arrogant attitude of one of the employees in the graphic art department. It embarrassed her to admit that she put off the *whole* project just because she dreaded interacting with this one man once in a while. She considered asking an administrative assistant to do the phoning and picking up in order to avoid having to communicate with this obnoxious guy, but eventually decided against it. Once she became aware of the difficulty, she resolved to handle it herself. She would make certain that she took care of all the graphics at the beginning of the day (to get the job over with), and if once in a while the dread of working with him was just too much, she'd ask for help from a coworker. The more Susan thought about it, the more she realized that she truly enjoyed doing the publicity. Today, it still amazes her that she had put it off just because of this one small aspect of the job.

The trick is to identify which aspect of a dreaded job is the part you hate and to use some creative problem solving to make that portion of your work a little less miserable.

WHAT ARE YOUR TROUBLE AREAS?

Some people procrastinate about everything in the world, but many procrastinate only about specific "trouble areas" of their lives. In fact, merely *thinking* of their trouble areas causes anxiety in some individuals.

To identify trouble areas, write down those tasks and jobs that fill you with dread. Trouble areas can be seasonal: taking down Christmas decorations, doing inventory, tackling the spring cleaning, working on the annual budget. Or they can be part of our everyday lives.

Helen, a manufacturer's rep who is now a recovering procrastinator, used to function fine at work, but her house (and much of her personal life) was in total chaos. Among her many trouble areas, one of the most troublesome at home had to do with sending out mail. She'd pour her heart into writing a letter to a friend and feel wonderful when it was finished. Then, three weeks later, it would still be sitting around the house because she hadn't yet found the address or tracked down an envelope and a stamp.

Eventually, she hit on a solution for this trouble area. Every time management and "getting organized" article she had ever read stressed the need for a desk. She didn't have an office—let alone a desk—and had always considered herself to be an exception to that rule. But as she concentrated on her trouble area, she realized that anything having to do with mailing out something would put her in a frenzied, frustrated state. Helen had previously thought her hatred of paying bills had something to do with spending money. Now she understood that the logistics of assembling the checkbook, bills, a pen, and stamps was the real culprit. So she decided to invest in a desk.

QUICK TIP

Buy what you need for those trouble areas.
Sometimes happiness is having an extra pair of
scissors or an extra $1.49 roll of tape.

"What a difference that little desk made!" she reports. "It became the control center for running our house. The desk contained large and small envelopes, stationery, addresses, pens, pencils, a pencil sharpener, stamps, scissors, tape—so many comforts of life."

Since using a desk made such a difference in her life, she plunged forward and bought a small, two-drawer filing cabinet. All the papers that used to accumulate in stacks around the house were now neatly filed. Helen says that her trouble area simply disappeared, and now she no longer dreads or puts off mailing letters or paying bills.

෧

In a Conquer Procrastination seminar, Larry explained that as a newspaper editor, he is an organized, efficient person, but his trouble area is keeping up with birthday cards and gifts for family and close friends. Larry just can't motivate himself to buy the gifts and cards, and when he finally does, they get lost somewhere in the house and never make it to the intended receiver. Eight other participants said they were in the same boat and were amazed to discover that they were not the only ones.

Once they started talking, the solution seemed simple: Designate one area for the gifts (perhaps a closet or, if they have children, a high closet shelf out of the reach of little ones) and one area for cards (maybe a drawer or shoebox). That way, cards and gifts won't end up all over the house and be forgotten, and when someone's birthday rolls around, they can go to one spot for the card, one spot for the gift, and their trouble area will be organized.

When my neighbor Leon decided to pinpoint his trouble area, he determined that he always procrastinated about repairing things around the house. After further thought, he identified the real problem: He could never find his tools when he needed them. So one summer, he put in some time and money building a workshop in his garage. He lined the walls with Peg-Board to hang his tools and even drew outlines around the tools so the whole family would know where they belonged when returning tools to the workshop. Admittedly, the tools don't always get hung up in their own special spots, but usually when Leon needs a tool, he'll find it in the workshop and he doesn't procrastinate about repair jobs nearly as much as he used to.

Greg, another seminar participant, found a simple solution to his trouble area at work. During discussions at business meetings, Greg would be asked to follow up on several projects. He'd leave the meeting with the best of intentions, but because he often did not take notes, or if he did, he'd jot something down on a scrap of paper then misplace it, he never did what he said he would do. At the next meeting, when asked if he'd followed up, Greg would make an excuse, and he would look and feel like the world's biggest procrastinator.

Finally, after being embarrassed numerous times, he took action: He set up a folder for each type of meeting, put a pad of paper in every folder so he could jot down all his assignments, developed a schedule for reviewing his notes, and made it a habit to bring his folder to every meeting he attended. The written assignment was his reminder, and follow-up became a simple habit.

Your trouble areas might be very different from these examples, but you get the idea. Once you identify your trouble area, do some brainstorming, and you'll think of ways to organize yourself or to set up systems to help you conquer these procrastination pitfalls.

THE POWER OF REWARDS

Another tip: Give yourself a reward—one that you'll really love—and let that reward motivate you to hurry up and finish the dreaded job. Make a list of rewards you enjoy and match them up to jobs you've been putting off. Use small rewards for small jobs, bigger rewards for bigger jobs. Examples of small rewards include a snack or a phone call to a friend. A big reward could be a trip to the zoo, a special purchase, or a night on the town.

Some people find it easy to reward themselves at the end of a project, and, as a result, they add enjoyment to their work by looking forward to the reward. Others are stumped. They can't think of a reward that would motivate them. They can't think of anything that they would enjoy. They don't know what relaxes them. This is partly because they have a work ethic that ties self-worth with the dictate "I am worthwhile only when I am being productive and working hard."

If you're having trouble coming up with rewards, I encourage you to start small. We're not talking about vacations to Hawaii. We're talking about simple, easy small rewards such as taking some time off to loaf or to do something with the family or a friend.

To keep from procrastinating and as a variation on a reward system, many people "deprive" themselves of a simple reward until a job is complete. If there's a new movie you're dying to see or a video you want to rent, push yourself to finish something, then relax and enjoy your reward—guilt free.

Kym, a college student, used to sit and stare at an assignment for three days before she would get started. (Once she started the project, however, she had no trouble finishing it.) Now she motivates herself through rewards. She will write or study for twenty minutes in absolute silence (which she hates) before turning on her favorite music.

Similarly, Bob had trouble beginning one of his daily tasks at the counseling center where he worked: Each morning he had to make a summary graph of the number and type of phone calls received during the previous night and then send it to the human resource director. It was a twenty-minute job. Unfortunately, Bob was a great procrastinator who'd take breaks when he wanted to put off something, and most days that graph was still incomplete and hanging over his head late into the afternoon. Thinking about it and dreading it all day long made Bob miserable.

When he finally conquered his procrastination, the weapon he used was coffee. Bob loved coffee with a passion, so his new routine became:

1. At home before work, he could drink all the coffee he wanted.
2. At work, no coffee till the graph was completed and sent to HR.

Within a month, Bob was in the habit of completing that graph during the first half hour at work. Once the graph was processed, he made a big deal of going for his

SOME REWARDS THAT MIGHT
MOTIVATE YOU TO GET
THE JOB DONE

ॐ

- enjoy a hobby
- attend a movie, play, or concert
- get a massage
- go shopping
- take an afternoon or full day off during your busy weekend
- attend a conference, seminar, or class
- get out of the office and go for a walk
- chat with friends or colleagues
- spend time outdoors in nature
- pamper yourself with extra sleep
- take time off to do nothing—without guilt
- spend time in the company of a loved one
- play a favorite sport or engage in some other type of physical exercise
- read a great book or magazine
- luxuriate in a bubble bath
- go fishing or hunting (alone or with friends)
- devote a whole evening to reading trashy magazines
- dine out
- do something absolutely useless just because you love doing it
- daydream
- go for a one-day or weekend retreat or other getaway

wonderful, delicious cup of coffee. Certainly, after a few months, doing the report first was a solid habit and he no longer needed to play the "reward game," but now—two years later—he still continues to postpone that first glorious cup of coffee until the dreaded graph is complete.

In one of my seminars, Jennifer told the following story: She had always wanted a spare room. But when her dream finally came true and she had a spare room, within no time at all, that room became the resting place and storage space for every stray item in her house.

One of her kids would ask, "Mom, where should I put this?"

Jennifer would reply, "Oh . . . I don't know . . . how about the spare room?"

Cleaning that room was one of her least favorite chores in the world. Stacks and stacks of clutter were everywhere because she didn't know where else to put all her stuff. She procrastinated about cleaning it because of what she called "The Spare Room Paradox: If I didn't know where to put things before, how am I supposed to figure out where to put everything now when I clean it?"

The solution: First, she started working on her attitude *before* she tackled the cleanup. Jennifer decided the payoff would be that every single time she passed it, she'd enjoy a neat, clean spare room and not be bombarded with guilt by all the mess cluttering up the place. Another payoff would be that when she needed something from that area, she wouldn't have to rummage through everything to find it.

Last but not least, she selected a wonderful reward. Jennifer told an understanding friend about how long she'd been putting off this job and how she needed to use every trick in the book (this book!) to motivate herself to clean that spare room. She and her friend decided to set aside a Sunday afternoon to go to their favorite art museum, but they solemnly agreed to cancel if Jennifer's goal of cleaning the spare room wasn't accomplished.

She borrowed a great set of audiotapes to play while she cleaned, sorted, stacked, packed, tossed out, recycled, and filed. Listening to the tapes made the time fly. And because she had set up a place to file the papers, and had found a charity that would accept most of her unwanted items, she wasn't stuck at the end of the job with stacks of things that didn't have a home.

The job was finished in a very short time. Jennifer enjoyed her reward. And most important, she could say that cleaning her spare room never overwhelmed her again because she had a strategy to help minimize the misery of doing the dreaded project.

Once you consciously start a reward system, it becomes habitual to push through a project so you can celebrate its completion with some kind of treat. For many of us, one of the very best rewards of all is time off. So work hard on your project; set a deadline; cut down on breaks; push yourself to complete the job. But when you finish, don't plunge right into another big job or a lot of little ones. Take some time off—to play, to relax, to have fun.

Within the word *recreation* is the idea that you can re-create yourself. Do something to refresh your spirit, to nurture the little kid in you, to re-create yourself physically, emotionally, or spiritually. Add some fun and some joy to your life. If you have nothing to look forward to at the end of the job except more work, why would you ever want to finish it?

What you're looking for are ways to make the dreaded job less horrendous, less overwhelming, and maybe even a bit pleasant, and to begin achieving whatever you need to move your life along in the right direction—the direction that *you* choose.

Thoughts to Consider

Whatever you do, don't let your progress go unnoticed—even if you are the only one who's noticing.

—Unknown

Lord help me to do with a smile those things I have to do anyway.

—Hal Roach

We do not stop playing because we grow old; we grow old because we stop playing.

—Unknown

You will never *find* time for anything. If you want time, you must *make* it.

—Charles Buxton

What gets rewarded gets done.

—Unknown

Unless each day can be looked back upon by an individual as one in which he has had some fun, some joy, some real satisfaction, that day is a loss.

—*Dwight D. Eisenhower*

Rest is not idleness, and to lie sometimes on the grass under the trees on a summer's day, listening to the murmur of water, or watching the clouds float across the sky, is by no means a waste of time.

—*Sir J. Lubbock*

In creating, the hardest part is
To begin.

—*Anonymous*

Tomorrow's fate, though thou be wise,
Thou canst not tell nor yet surmise;
Pass, therefore, not today in vain,
For it will never come again.

—*Omar Khayyam*

⊸⌒

EXTRA CREDIT

Make a list of little and big rewards (which you can provide) to motivate yourself to do a task or job that you tend to put off:

• Little Rewards (for completing little jobs) _____

_____

• Big Rewards (for completing big jobs) _____

_____

• Great Fabulous Rewards (for completing life-changing accomplishments) _____

_____

Don't kid yourself by saying, "Completing the job is reward enough." If that were true, why would you put it off in the first place?

EXTRA, EXTRA CREDIT

(Not to worry. It's easy stuff.)

1. Buy a timer.
2. Select one task to do that you've been putting off.
3. Set the timer for one hour.
4. Work at that task. No breaks.
5. Pat yourself on the back.

2

What's Your
Excuse?

❧

IN MY CONQUER PROCRASTINATION seminars, I ask participants to clarify their own personal, specific procrastination pitfalls by writing out a list of 101 things that they've been meaning to do but never get around to. They either carry the 101 list with them or post it where they can see it every day. Then, as they encounter my examples, they can refer to the list and apply the ideas to their specific procrastination problems.

During the process of making the list (it usually takes several days), I encourage them to walk around their workspace, then through their houses, looking slowly and carefully at each area. They scroll through their computers, go through closets, cabinets, and other storage areas. On the list they put everything they can think of that needs to be . . .

checked out	changed
returned	removed

repaired	waxed
cleaned	put away
altered	organized
replaced	converted
moved	taken out
tossed out	remodeled
modified	reorganized
washed	deleted
painted	finished
decluttered	purchased

The 101 list is not limited to a walk-through around the house and work area. In addition, people are encouraged to think through various aspects of their lives: physical, mental, and spiritual health; social and civic organizations; friends, family, and pets. They can add anything and everything they think of that they've been meaning to do "someday."

Also, it's not a "once in a lifetime" exercise. The list constantly changes. Anytime you start feeling overwhelmed with things to do, you need to write that list. As long as everything is floating around in your head, you can't think straight, and soon guilt and anxiety muddle your thinking. Most people report that just the act of writing out the list results in their taking care of one or several of the items within a day or two.

Miserable, Mealymouthed Excuses

As you write your list, you may notice all kinds of excuses popping up. I can relate. We hear these excuses every day. "My life would be better if I did ————, but I'm too old, too young, too busy, too unskilled, too uneducated, too weak willed, too scared . . ." The list goes on forever.

Every time you voice excuses, you are trying to convince someone (most often yourself) that it's OK that you did or didn't do something. You may have noticed that excuses undermine other people's confidence in you, but are you aware that excuses harm your self-esteem? For every excuse you say out loud, you yourself hear it and, worse, believe it. Each new excuse you believe and accept becomes another self-limit that inhibits you. When you start stacking up limits or accepting excuses, you're putting obstacles in the way of becoming a more fully functioning person.

JoAnn had talked her whole adult life about how much she wished she'd gone to college, but there was always a reason (excuse) that kept her from realizing this goal: She couldn't afford it; she had to raise her family; she was too busy with her career; she had no time. Her latest excuse was that she was too old. The last time her husband suggested she go to college, JoAnn told him, "If I start now part-time, I'll be sixty when I graduate."

He told her, "You'll be sixty anyway. You can be sixty with or without a college degree." She finally stopped making excuses and enrolled in college. She thought she'd be exhausted working all day and taking classes at night and on weekends, but she says she's never felt more energized.

Do you have some excuses, some self-limits, that are so strong they have become a part of your basic philosophy of life? Do you believe you procrastinate because you were born this way? Or because you think you are too stupid or disorganized or weak or (fill in the blank) to change?

TAKE CONTROL OF YOUR SELF-TALK

All these excuses, these self-limits, come from the way you talk to yourself. It's time to turn self-talk into something positive.

For example, each generation of women in my family was brought up to believe we aren't mechanically inclined, which became a phrase we repeated to ourselves and others at every opportunity. As I worked on "converting" from being a procrastinator, I started to take charge of my self-talk and decided to begin blasting away at some of my excuses. One place to start was this supposed helplessness around machinery.

Within a week of that decision, I was leaving for work on a cold, Chicago winter morning, when my car wouldn't start. The teenage boy next door came out and said, "Don't worry, Mrs. Emmett, you just flooded it. I can fix it by sticking a pen in the butterfly valve."

I said to myself, "Butterfly valve? I like butterflies. I

bet I could learn this!" So I explained to him my new resolution.

He said, "Sure, I can teach you. It's easy. Just open the hood."

"You don't understand the extent of my limitation," I replied sheepishly. "I don't know how to open the hood."

So he patiently showed me, then taught me how to find the right valve and where to place the ballpoint pen. The car started! Together we removed the pen, closed the hood, and I was on my way to ending my legacy of limitations.

The next day, I was taking my daughter, Kerry, and four of her teen girlfriends to the movies. We all piled into the car, and, again, it wouldn't start. As my heart started to sink, I heard a voice inside my head say, "Come on, Rita, get some positive talk going. You know how to fix this." So I gave myself a silent, quick pep talk, then I confidently—no, boldly—stepped out and walked to the front of the car, opened the hood, and jammed a pen into the butterfly valve.

I slid back behind the steering wheel, held my breath, turned the ignition key, and the car started up. Five teenage girls, including my daughter, cheered me. My self-esteem was soaring.

Over the next few years, I continued giving positive messages to myself, and gradually I became more confident around mechanical things. This confidence spilled over at work. Our executive director announced that he wanted someone to learn to run the new video equipment and was told, "Ask Rita Emmett. She's mechanically inclined." Maybe someone had seen me in the parking lot fixing an employee's car. I'd become a whiz with a ballpoint pen. So I said, "I don't know how to run video equipment, but I'll learn." And I did.

I also stopped putting off all the other things I'd always wanted to learn about but had thought I couldn't because "I wasn't mechanically inclined." I became the first adult on our block who could program a VCR. When home computers came on the scene, I listened to other people's excuses and anxieties, but I was past that, so I jumped right in.

Eventually, I traded in my old car for a newer model. At some point, it wouldn't start, so I opened the hood and discovered that the new, improved cars no longer have butterfly valves. I panicked. "What if I lose all my mechanical ability? What if I go to work and I can't operate the video equipment anymore?"

Of course, that didn't happen. I've never gone back to assuming I'm not good with mechanical things. Once those limits are knocked down, they generally stay down.

As long as people believe they cannot do something, they usually cannot. Ah, but watch out for the ones who believe they *can* do something. The old saying "What the mind can conceive and believe, it can achieve" holds a great deal of power for procrastinators.

Each time you begin to procrastinate, give yourself a pep talk. Replace your excuses with affirming messages that you can achieve what you want. By reading the quotes at the end of each chapter, you can find some favorite positive statements to copy and stick on your wall or phone or dashboard to counteract all the negative ones we hear from others or—worse—from ourselves.

It's time to stop accepting your own excuses. It doesn't matter how long you've been considered a procrastinator. What does matter is that you can change. And you don't have to put it off until tomorrow. You can start changing right now. This minute.

THE MOTHER OF ALL EXCUSES: "I WORK BEST UNDER PRESSURE"

Do you procrastinate because you believe you work best under pressure?

But what do you mean when you say you work best under pressure? Do you mean that as you near a deadline, your adrenaline starts pumping, your energy soars, your efforts become more focused and effective, and—feeling calm and confident—you do a good job, finishing on time? If the answer is yes, there is no problem . . . unless you also answer yes to any of the next questions:

- At deadline time, do you feel stressed and pressured? Frazzled and fragmented? Chaotic and crazy?
- Do you feel that you have 100 things to do and no time left in which to do them?
- Do you sometimes cry for help, enlisting family, friends, or coworkers to bail you out?
- Are you generating stress for everyone around you? (If

you're not certain, ask a few people if they feel like strangling you at deadline time.)

- As the deadline draws near, do you have headaches, stomachaches, backaches, foot aches, or other ailments?
- Do you sometimes miss the deadline?
- Are you crabby and cranky and irritable and mean and nasty under deadline pressures?

If you answer yes to one or more of these questions, you aren't really doing your best work under pressure.

Rick, who wrote grant applications at a not-for-profit organization, blithely tripped through life leaving everything until the last minute. He loved telling people he worked best under pressure. The problem was that he drove his coworkers crazy when he was under pressure, and his wife and kids threatened to pack up and leave the house when he was on deadline. His idea of "working best under pressure" was that he turned into a monster who was impossible to live or work with.

Many people who claim to "work best under pressure" simply don't. Under pressure, they might:

- fall apart
- act or feel crazy
- lose sleep
- yell at, nag, or criticize others
- overeat or eat too little
- become stressed
- do a hurried, sloppy, or incomplete job
- burn out
- make others crazy
- become sick
- miss an important deadline.

But none of these are conditions under which a person "works best."

A more truthful way to explain this situation would be: "I can't get myself to do anything until the pressure of a deadline arrives; then I really get to work." The key to conquering this "I Work Best Under Pressure" procrastination is to change your attitude.

At the end of a daylong Conquer Procrastination seminar, Ramish approached me and summed up the situation: "I've always said that I work best under pressure. Not true. What I do is coast along, taking the easy way, the lazy way, out. Then, when the pressure starts, I get to work.

"I don't do my best work under pressure; I don't even

do good work when I leave everything until the last minute. Something usually goes wrong—a crisis, sickness, emergency, something! Then I say that I would have done it better if this didn't happen."

Certainly, I admit that some projects can be left to the last minute without making us crazy. The trick is to evaluate the situation ahead of time and consider the consequences you'll have to pay if you don't make the deadline or if you have to complete the task more quickly than you'd like.

Here's an example: You are expecting company in a few days and your place needs to be cleaned. You could start now, but you decide to leave everything until the last-minute pressure hits.

Now the law of averages dictates that if you leave everything until the last minute, something is likely to go wrong. You have to work late, you have car trouble, a toothache lands you in the dentist's office; something—anything—can happen to prevent you from cleaning your home.

In this instance, the consequences really aren't so terrible. Your company arrives, and your place is a mess. You might be a little embarrassed, but you'll survive without severe repercussions. There's no problem with this situation and no reason you couldn't leave your housecleaning until the last minute.

However, in a different situation, the consequences might be much more serious. For example: You have an important report to write at work; your boss is counting on it, and you decide that because "you work best under pressure," you'll leave everything until the last minute. Inevitably, Murphy's Law kicks into gear; this law states that anything that can go wrong will go wrong. So you get the world's worst case of flu or a snowstorm keeps you from getting to work. You have to confess to your boss that not only is the report not complete, it isn't even begun.

Now consider the consequences.

You may have jeopardized your job, or made your boss look bad, or blown your chances for that promotion you were counting on, or at the very minimum, you may have lowered your boss's evaluation of your worth to the company—all because of a habit of putting off things due to the rationalization that you work best under pressure.

What is the price you've had to pay for leaving things until the last minute? Can you remember times when your heart was pounding because you waited until the last minute to leave for a meeting, and you ended up sitting in your car, stuck in a traffic jam?

After you've acknowledged that you need to change

your attitude, use the success strategies in part III to break up projects into manageable tasks and control your time so these deadlines are no longer the source of panic, sickness, craziness, and mediocrity.

IS IT EVER GOOD TO PROCRASTINATE?

Now, here's a surprise: under certain circumstances, you actually *should* put something off till later. I truly believe you can conquer procrastination, but I also believe there are times when you should say, "I'm not going to fight this one. I'm putting it off."

Everyone procrastinates at one time or another. We need to choose our battles; we can't do everything. There are some things we should put off—consciously, purposefully. I call this Positive Procrastination.

Parkinson's Law states that work expands to fill the time available for its completion. We've all experienced this. If company's coming and you have two days to clean the house, it takes two solid days of cleaning. But if you have only four hours to clean the house, you get it sparkling clean in four hours. (Well, perhaps not exactly "sparkling.")

How does this law apply to Positive Procrastination? Some people deliberately delay cleaning the house until four hours before their guests are expected, simply because they don't want to devote two whole days of their lives to putting the place in order.

The same law applies to writing. Some people will write an article, letter, whatever, and will rewrite endlessly until they are crawling out of their skin.

These compulsive revisers do themselves a favor by putting off the writing until they have a comfortable enough margin to get it done well, but not so much time that they're rewriting for weeks. (No, this does not mean that you should wait until the last nanosecond and then turn in work you didn't have time to revise or even proofread.)

Positive Procrastination applies to many aspects of our lives. Creativity, for instance. When I have a really great idea, I find I'm better off letting it simmer awhile. I set it on the back burner of my brain and just let it cook, while I deliberately get involved in something else.

An art director once told me that sometimes when she's working on a design, she'll spend hours without getting anywhere. Rather than keep trying, she'll work on something else for a day or two. When she comes back to the original design project, she sees it from a different perspective and will be more successful than if she persevered. When you are feeling stale or blocked with a project, put it aside, let it incubate, and see if coming back later for a fresh start doesn't revitalize both you and the project.

We get into trouble when we put off something for no good reason. However, once in a while, there is a good reason for Positive Procrastination.

THOUGHTS TO CONSIDER

That which the fool does in the end, the wise man does in the beginning.

—R. C. Tench

If you always do what you've always done, you'll always get what you've always got.

—Anonymous

Nothing is so fatiguing as the eternal hanging on of an uncompleted task.

—William James

Whether you think you can or you think you can't, you're right!

—Henry Ford

EMMETT'S OBSERVATION: God created company so the house would get cleaned.

—Rita Emmett

The more I want to get something done, the less I call it work.

—Richard Bach

Time is not measured by the passing of years but by what one does, how one feels, and what one achieves.

—Unknown

Humans need order in their lives to function at their best. The order of our days in many ways gives us our images of ourselves.

—*L. Tornabene*

Remember that lost time does not return.

—*Thomas à Kempis*

Time wasted is existence; time used is life.

—*Edward Young*

EXTRA CREDIT

List 101 things you need (or want) to do. (Countless times, I've heard stories of people locked out of their house or car, who say, "I meant to make an extra key." If you don't have a spare key, add that to your to-do list. Next, find a great hiding place for your key, and remember where you hid it.)

3

The Games
People Play

꿍

PROCRASTINATION IS A GAME—a game of
putting off, ignoring, forgetting, simply not thinking
about what you want to avoid doing. And one way many
people play the game is by practicing what I call Hypocritical Procrastination. It is employed when you have
something important to do, that you need to do, must do,
or you'll be in big trouble.

But you don't want to do it.

You can't put it off by simply being lazy, because the
task is too important. No, you couldn't face yourself or
others if you procrastinated for no good reason; so you put
it off by doing something noble instead.

Let me give you an example. Back in my procrastination days, I was assigned the job of typing a roster for a
committee I served on. I hate to type. I never took a typing course, so I use the biblical method: "Seek and ye shall
find." I make a lot of mistakes and then get frustrated and

angry. After working on the roster for a while, I wandered into the kitchen to get a cup of coffee. Heading back to my dreaded typing chore, I noticed something purple on the kitchen wall—maybe grape jelly, surely grape something. I had no idea how long it had been there. I grabbed a bottle of cleanser and squirted that purple blob right off the wall. The result? A very bright, very obvious, very clean spot on my not-so-clean kitchen wall. I tried to blend in that clean spot with the rest of the wall; I figured if I "feathered" the dirt just right, I could eliminate that line of demarcation. It didn't work. So I poured the cleanser into a bucket and washed all the kitchen walls and ceiling. That evening, a committee member called to ask me how the typing was going.

"How could I type that roster when I've spent all day scrubbing the kitchen walls and ceiling?" I said, hypocritically. I couldn't have faced myself or anyone else if I had put off my typing duty in order to watch TV or take a nap, but it was OK because I had been busy doing something else that was, uh, important.

VARIATIONS OF HYPOCRITICAL PROCRASTINATION

Most of us play this game of Hypocritical Procrastination quite unconsciously, and we have endless variations. One group of people, whom I call the Travelers, react to a task

Thirteen "Hypocritical" Time-Wasting Games

1. Shuffling through the same papers or clutter over and over.
2. Playing computer games.
3. Having long, chatty telephone calls that aren't important to you.
4. Lingering with unexpected visitors who aren't important to you.
5. Surfing the Web.
6. Attending unnecessary meetings.
7. Working aimlessly without objectives, priorities, or deadlines.
8. Trying to do too many things at once and underestimating the time available to do them all.
9. Being indecisive.
10. Saying yes when you should be saying no.
11. Pushing yourself when you're too tired to function well.
12. Doing things that don't need to be done (or that somebody else could do).
13. Doing an excessive amount of preparation.

by remembering they have some very important chores to do elsewhere. Or they travel elsewhere hoping to find some very important chores to do. An uncontrollable urge moves them away from the work to be done. They will travel anywhere: to the coffeepot, to the fax machine, to the basement, to the stockroom, to the garage, to the mailbox. If they're near an elevator, they'll take it up or down. If they're near a window, they'll open or close it. If they're near a pencil, they'll travel till they find a place to sharpen it. If they're near food, they'll eat. If they're not near food, they'll keep traveling until they land near food, then they'll eat.

They pace; they wander; they walk. And when their roaming brings them back to the task at hand, the traveling bug bites them again, and off they go.

Some Hypocritical Procrastinators fall into the group I call Perfect Preparers. They decide they simply cannot work on this project until they've done more research, obtained more information, read more books, attended more seminars. You can become so good at this that you actually spend years preparing to start a project. This is OK if you're putting off building a backyard deck, but if you work in sales and don't call on your accounts because you're waiting for the next quarterly report, being a Perfect Preparer may cost your company the sale and you the commission, if not your job.

Then there are the Socializers. The mere thought of doing an undesirable task reminds them to call friends and relatives they haven't thought about in years. Or to have an in-depth discussion with their spouse. Or to E-mail their pen pal in Australia. At work, Socializers visit coworkers, wandering from desk to desk, station to station, office to office just to put off whatever it is they don't want to do.

Straighteners are those who suddenly decide that quality work cannot possibly be accomplished in messy working conditions. So they straighten and organize and rearrange and dust and throw away and vacuum and file until they can look at the clock and mumble, "Well, it's too late to start that project today. Guess I'll have to wait till tomorrow."

Finally, there are the Happy Helpers, who practice the most subtle and insidious style of Hypocritical Procrastination. They put aside work they should do—but don't want to do—in order to help someone . . . whether that person needs their help or not. Note that if the person actually *needs* their help, it isn't procrastination, but rather the fulfilling of a valid need. It's only a coincidence that the Happy Helpers get to put off whatever it is they don't want to do while they lovingly help relatives, friends, coworkers, neighbors, or even strangers. But often, Happy Helpers are actually being manipulated by people whose needs are not valid.

Beware of people who are experts at convincing you that *you* are in charge of their problems. They start by subtly asking for a favor. Consider, for example, the coworker who asks you to help him with his project. When you explain that you are swamped, he panics and insists that if he doesn't have it done by the deadline, he might lose his job.

The expectation is that you will bail him out; but what happens when *your* work is not accomplished?

I'm not advocating that you stop helping your family or friends. But be careful when others put you in charge of their problems. Your help could be preventing them from growing and becoming more responsible; meanwhile, you delay getting your own work done, thus creating problems for yourself. You may be lying awake at night worrying about other people's problems, while they are snuggled in bed sound asleep, carefree, because they've passed their concerns over to you.

Stick a sign on your forehead (or desk) that says:

Lack of planning on *your* part does not
constitute an emergency on *my* part.

At times, Happy Helpers abandon their projects to rush off and help others because their own projects seem boring or unpleasant compared to the newness and excitement of other people's jobs. Furthermore, it feels good to lend a helping hand. Everyone wants to be liked, and people usually are grateful when you pitch in and do their work for them.

Some Happy Helpers just don't know how to say no to a request for help. They want to be "nice guys." They can't stand being thought of as mean or selfish or uncaring. They want to be liked. Their self-esteem is based on other people thinking kindly of them. Of course, if they are surrounded by negative, mean people who are users, the Happy Helpers can never do enough, or they feel they are never good enough.

They don't want to say no and hurt the other person's feelings. But we've all had experience with people politely refusing our requests:

- "I'd love to help you move to your new place, but I can't. I'm busy that weekend."
- "Sorry, I can't talk with you now; I'm tied up. OK if I call you later?"
- "I'd like to pitch in on that computer project with you, but I'm just swamped with work, and I'm racing against a deadline. You'll have to ask someone else this time."

When people say no to us, we don't declare an end to our friendship or stop speaking to them. So why assume that others will stop liking us when we occasionally refuse their requests?

Many Happy Helpers will say that they are happiest when helping others. Perhaps that's true, but a problem may exist no matter how happy a person is. If you regret all the work you're putting aside while you help others, if helping others means that you're neglecting your family or yourself, or that you're not finishing work you were hired to do, then it's time to assert yourself and to occasionally say no to other people's requests. To always say yes to requests can lead to exhaustion, resentment, and downright hostility. The Irish poet William Butler Yeats wrote:

> *Too long a sacrifice*
> *Can make a stone of the heart.*

You can become assertive and still remain a kind, loving, polite human being—and get your work done, too.

DRIFTING ALONG

Some Hypocritical Procrastinators practice the art of "drifting." It's not like being a ship without a rudder; it's more like being a ship without a destination. Have you ever looked back over the past morning or afternoon or evening without having a clue what you did or where the time went? Some drifters start several jobs and never finish any; others putter around without really doing anything.

Drifting occurs under a variety of circumstances: when you feel depressed, overwhelmed, distracted, or excited, or when you haven't planned what to do with your time. It usually occurs during unstructured time.

If you were living a day of totally structured time, you would know the precise moment to wake up in the morning, when to eat breakfast, and when to leave for work.

SO WHAT DO YOU CALL A NONPROCRASTINATOR?

Hard as it is to believe, you were most likely born *not* a procrastinator but a . . . what? What do you call people who don't put things off? What's the opposite of a procrastinator?

You can't call them achievers or leaders, or label them as organized or motivated, because we all know people who, in spite of being organized achievers or motivated leaders, still continue to procrastinate in many areas of their lives.

I don't like the word *nonprocrastinator*, because it doesn't differentiate between people who have no tendency to procrastinate and those who have fought and won the battle against procrastination. Putting the prefix *non* before a word doesn't tell you much. For example, nonsmokers could be people who never smoked, or who quit years ago, or who just quit last week and are carrying around pictures of black lungs to show to all their smoking friends.

The Latin word *crastinus* means "of tomorrow." In that case, procrastinators are in favor of crastinating (or putting off till tomorrow), so their opposite would be anticrastinators.

You might start work at 9:00 A.M., take a coffee break at 10:30 A.M., eat lunch at noon, take another break at 3:30 P.M., and leave work at 5:00 P.M. At home in the evening, you would eat dinner, start watching TV, then go to bed, all at certain specified times. You don't usually find yourself drifting during a highly structured day; it's a day of "anticrastination."

Now let's flip the coin and imagine a day of totally unstructured time. No alarm goes off because you have nothing planned. You get out of bed whenever you want; there's no reason to get dressed. You hope the phone will ring soon, so you'll have an idea if anything is going to happen today.

Most of us live our days somewhere in between these extremes. Or we bounce from fairly structured workdays to fairly unstructured weekends. Some people function fine regardless of whether their time is structured or unstructured; others deal better with one than the other. Many high achievers, who never, ever procrastinate during the structured time at work, fall into patterns of "drifting" (and procrastinating) during unstructured time at home.

Some occupations are particularly unstructured, such as homemakers, clergy, and real estate and insurance agents. Those who work out of their homes also have to contend with unstructured time. All these people must be particularly vigilant to guard against drifting. In every occupation, it seems as if some areas are more unstructured than others. For example, in the field of law, probate lawyers often don't have the same urgency or type of deadlines that most other lawyers have. Because of this lack of urgency, it is easy for probate lawyers to obtain extensions and therefore to procrastinate. Unstructured occupations call for more target deadlines, more planning, more dedication to list making and prioritizing, and definitely more anticrastinating than a more structured situation might require.

The beginning of a cure for drifting is to recognize it: "Eureka! I'm drifting." The next step is to get yourself in gear and finish one task. As the saying goes, "Success breeds success."

By the same token, "Failure breeds failure." Looking back at a block of time spent on uncompleted tasks can make you feel like a failure and, sometimes, cause you to act like one. In addition, uncompleted tasks can create more work. For example, in a Conquer Procrastination seminar, Mary said her fat, grumpy cat loved to lie in freshly washed and dried laundry. If she didn't put away the clothes before the cat got to them, Mary not only had to wash everything over again but also felt like a loser for procrastinating about putting away the newly washed items.

Drifting is a style of procrastination that wastes time and prevents us from getting things done; it also undermines our sense of self-worth, leaving us feeling stupid and disorganized. Watch out for it. Catch yourself when you're drifting. Turn yourself around by finishing one task. Then another. Then another.

Overcoming Hypocritical Procrastination

The key to eliminating Hypocritical Procrastination is to start recognizing this type of procrastination in your life. Become aware of the games you (we all) play. Once you become conscious of your style of Hypocritical Procrastination, you can watch for it: You realize that you're cleaning out desk drawers when you planned on calling and expressing your sympathy to an acquaintance, or that you're rearranging the linen closet when you promised yourself you'd exercise, meditate, or write in your journal, or that you're playing a computer game when something important needs to be done.

Hypocritical Procrastination and all its variations have one characteristic in common: *lack of focus.* Once you start to focus by setting a deadline for a task or making a commitment and writing it on a to-do list, the other "important" things to do, which generate this type of procrastination, tend to fall away.

Power Plays: Personal and Professional

Another subtle but insidious procrastination game is Rebellious Procrastination. Whether they realize their motives or not, people who feel powerless or inadequate sometimes stage quiet little rebellions in the form of procrastination.

Here is an example: A wife points out to her husband some needed repairs around the house. He says, "Sure, I'll take care of everything this weekend." He knows that later he can turn her into a frustrated, furious woman— not by refusing to do the repairs, not by objecting, not by starting a fight, but by simply not doing what he promised.

His ability to manipulate his wife's emotions by procrastinating gives him a sense of power. Subconsciously, he exercises control over her without expending any energy whatsoever. But there are many layers to the consequences he will have to pay, from the obvious (a house that looks like it's falling apart) to the more subtle (a wife who is filled with resentment from his nonloving behavior in their relationship).

Another example: Pedro, who attended my Conquer Procrastination seminar, said that when he was promoted to supervisor, several of his coworkers resented it and were showing their resentment through procrastination. Three months after the seminar, he told me: "I know that this was their problem, not mine, but it felt like they were trying to sabotage me. Now I've started to ease up on the control I have over my department. I ask their opinions more often, give more responsibility, involve people more in the decision-making process; I guess I'm a bit friendlier.

"It's incredible. My staff does a lot less rebelling now. The procrastination has practically disappeared. It's magic."

Look at the amount of control a coworker has when he or she procrastinates on a report. If the report isn't ready by deadline, a whole department, perhaps the whole company, can be thrown into chaos.

Rebellious Procrastination is extremely harmful because, even though you hurt the one you are rebelling against, you hurt yourself so much more. You miss deadlines and establish a reputation of being a "do nothing" because you work hard at doing nothing. Procrastination not only leaves you with unfinished tasks but also erodes your self-esteem, your sense of being a worthwhile person. What a futile, destructive way to try to exercise control over others.

Some people who practice Rebellious Procrastination will recognize that they have been subconsciously rebelling against one or both of their parents, even parents who have passed away years ago. Start exploring the reasons for your own rebellion. Do you feel you have little or no control in certain relationships or situations? Does your procrastination cause upset or anger or some form of chaos? Do you achieve a sense of control or power when you put things off?

The first step to conquering Rebellious Procrastination is to find some other way of gaining control in your life. Acknowledge problems you may be having with people at home or at work. Communicate your concerns directly to those parties. Set goals for yourself. Use the tips in this book to change your procrastinating ways. You'll be amazed at the freedom you'll experience. By taking positive action, anticrastinators often enjoy a feeling of success and power, which far exceeds the sense of control achieved by rebellion and procrastination.

If you are unable to curb Rebellious Procrastination on your own, it's a good idea to seek counseling. This rebellion may be so deep within the subconscious that help from a professional might be required.

ARE WE BORN THIS WAY?

I used to think that I was born a procrastinator and, therefore, could never change. But after I married and our kids were born, I started to notice something. When babies want to do something, they want to do it now—immediately! They wail at the top of their lungs, rattling the whole house in an attempt to get what they want. During the first few years of their lives, children are slowly and subtly (and probably unconsciously) taught to become either procrastinators or anticrastinators.

Elizabeth, an investigator for the police department, told me this story about her daughter, Meghan. When Meghan was two years old, she watched a family on TV that was going on a picnic and then asked if their family could have a picnic. Elizabeth agreed but explained they'd have to wait until summer because, at that moment, the ground was covered with snow and the temperature was below zero. Meghan immediately began planning the picnic: Over the next few days, she collected a blanket, a picnic basket, and a thermos for juice. That little girl talked about the picnic so frequently and so enthusiastically that one evening as Elizabeth's family gathered for dinner, they were greeted by a blanket spread out on the living room floor. They had their picnic. It was indoors, but it was great.

If Elizabeth had insisted on waiting until summer to have the picnic, she inadvertently (and with the best of intentions) might have sowed the seeds of procrastination in Meghan.

I don't believe children—or anyone, for that matter—should receive instant gratification for everything they want. And much of what children want to do *now* simply cannot be done now, so we have no choice but to tell them, "Later." Still, I am convinced that we are born with a spirit of enthusiasm for wanting to do things *now*, and somewhere along the way we learn to make excuses and to put things off until tomorrow.

෨

THOUGHTS TO CONSIDER

Anyone can do any amount of work, provided it isn't the work he or she is supposed to be doing at the moment.

—*Robert Benchley*

It is not enough to be busy; so are the ants. The question is: What are we busy about?

—*Henry David Thoreau*

Beware the barrenness of a too busy life.

—Socrates

Live Life Today! This is NOT a dress rehearsal.

—Unknown

It's not hard to make decisions when you know what your values are.

—Roy Disney

Don't put off for tomorrow what you can do today, because if you enjoy it today you can do it again tomorrow.

—James A. Michener

Procrastination is opportunity's natural assassin.

—Victor Kiam

Lost, yesterday,
somewhere between sunrise and sunset,
two golden hours,
each set with sixty diamond minutes.
No reward is offered
for they are gone forever.

—Horace Mann

God has promised forgiveness to your repentance, but He has not promised tomorrow to your procrastination.

—St. Augustine

EXTRA CREDIT

1. Are you spending any of your time doing things you don't want to do, going places you don't want to go, and/or being with people you don't want to be with? If so, are you doing this simply because you can't say no? (Or, worse yet, nobody asked but you offered to do it without thinking?)

   • List the situations. _____

   _____

2. Are there any relationships in your life where you repeatedly say yes, then you "forget" to do what was promised?

   • List those relationships. _____

   _____

   • What changes can you make so you don't feel so powerless? _____

   _____

   • Select one relationship. Try explaining to the other party why you don't want to do what you were asked to do. _____

   _____

EXTRA, EXTRA CREDIT

This week, say no to a request to do something that is not necessary and that interferes with your own plans or that the other person should do for himself or herself.

PART II

Why We Procrastinate

4

The Fears That Stop You Cold

Emmett's Second Law: Obsession with perfection is the downfall of procrastinators.

THERE ARE DOZENS OF fears that can immobilize you and cause you to procrastinate. What do you do if a fear brings you to a screeching halt? The most effective way to strip these ghosts of the power they hold over you is to look them squarely in the face. Identify them. Put a name to them. The better you know them and the more clearly you see them, the less frightening they will seem.

In this chapter we'll take a look at some of the fears that are standing in your way.

FEAR OF IMPERFECTION

You may not think of yourself as a perfectionist, but do you put off things until the time or the mood or conditions are just right? Betty, who attended one of my seminars, re-marked, "Well, I'm certainly not a perfectionist; my house and car are always a mess." Yet she'll delay writing a letter until she has a nice big chunk of time when she will be in-spired to write with the eloquence of Shakespeare.

Similarly, Jane and Bill talked for months, even years, about setting up a financial investment plan but never did anything about it. They came up with all kinds of reasons and excuses, because subconsciously they feared setting up an imperfect plan.

For entirely different reasons, Shayna has been putting off getting a medical or dental checkup. She's in good health, and isn't afraid of the checkup, but she fears that setting up an appointment for a month from now might interfere with an important meeting at work or the arrival of out-of-town guests.

And so it goes. People wait until they are in the right mood, have the ideal amount of time, the best conditions . . . and unless all those "perfect" factors come together, decisions, actions, beginnings, endings, moves, purchases, relationships, careers, and lives are put on hold.

One important lesson in conquering procrastination is to realize that these perfect situations may never come. This is an imperfect world and we are imperfect people. Mind you, I'm not saying aim for mediocrity. Shoot for ex-cellence. It's achievable. Perfection usually isn't.

People who have succeeded in any area can tell you that you have to accept falling short of your goal as a nec-essary step toward achieving success. Michael Jordan, former Chicago Bulls basketball star, is quoted on a poster saying: "I've missed more than 9,000 shots in my career. I've lost almost 300 games. Twenty-six times I've been trusted to make the game-winning shot and missed. I've failed over and over and over again in my life. So that is why I succeed."

If your goal is to set up a financial investment plan, do some homework to come up with the best plan you can. Give yourself a deadline for starting to implement your plan instead of searching indefinitely for the *perfect* plan. When it's time to write a letter or finish a project or draw up a will or ask for a raise, you can plan on doing the best job possible. But realize it probably won't be perfect.

Stella Conquers Her Perfectionism

Stella, an executive director of a suburban chamber of commerce, was a perfectionist before making an amazing turnaround in her office and her life. Friends and coworkers noted that she'd stopped procrastinating and became the personification of productivity and efficiency, and they asked how she did it.

Stella gave the credit to her husband, Ed, a general contractor, who taught her a new way of self-talk. He became so frustrated with Stella's perfectionism that one day he drove her out to one of his job sites and showed her some of the beautiful work his carpenters did—bookcases, cabinets, hardwood floors, and a magnificent built-in corner entertainment unit. Stella sincerely admired the work and said, "This is all so beautiful. These workers are perfectionists."

"No, they're not," Ed said, "although God knows, when carpenters make a mistake, usually everyone sees it and gives them a hard time. They're not perfectionists, but they *do* have a standard of excellence. Almost every carpenter in the country knows that you have to measure twice and cut once. Making mistakes when you cut can be *very* expensive.

"On the other hand, even though they measure twice, sometimes there's a mistake. And do you know what they say to themselves when they goof up?"

"What?" asked Stella.

"'It ain't a grand piano.'" Ed explained, "You see, not everything a carpenter does is going to be at the same level of importance as a grand piano. Sometimes when something is less than perfect, it can still be excellent, so you can live with it."

This way of talking to yourself really clicked with Stella. She began to stop putting off difficult phone calls, paperwork, decisions; she became an anticrastinator.

Recently, Ed called her to see if she'd be home for dinner and she told him, "Sure will! I'm doing the work of three people here, and I haven't finished a third of what I need to before the October meeting, but that's OK. I'm coming home now anyway because the stuff I haven't completed yet just ain't a grand piano."

There was a time in my life when I was an avid perfectionist. I put off everything till the circumstance or time was perfect. I'm surprised my friends and family didn't abandon me, with all the unreasonable expectations I dumped on them and on myself. Then something happened when I was a Cub Scout den leader that turned my thinking upside down.

Our den consisted of six boys, including twins named Pat and Mike. When we made gifts for the moms and dads, these twins were constantly looking over each other's shoulder to make sure their gifts were identical.

One year we made stained-glass ornaments for Christmas gifts. On a cookie sheet, each boy placed a metal outline of a shape such as a snowman or a star, then filled the frame with plastic beads that would melt in a hot oven and look like stained glass. By the end of the meeting at 5:00 P.M., the boys had completed everything except the baking of the beads. I told them that if they were late for dinner, their parents would worry, so I'd bake the ornaments in the oven when they left, and they could come the next day after school to pick up the finished present.

To this day, I don't know what went wrong, but when I took out the ornaments, I saw that the beads had bounced around and gotten mixed up in five of the six little metal frames. I frantically tried to scrape a melted green blob from Pat's white snowman. It didn't work. Five ornaments were ruined, one was perfect; it was Mike's. The twins' gifts didn't match.

I called my friend Julie and explained how the boys had worked so hard and now five of the Christmas gifts were ruined. What would I say to them the next day when they came to pick up their creations?

Instead of offering advice, Julie told me the story of how certain Native American artists deliberately put a flaw in their beadwork to remind them that only God is perfect—we are imperfect people. Julie also told me that many quilters have a tradition of putting a flaw in hand-made quilts—for the same reason. After our conversation, I went to the library and took out a book with photos of Native American belts and other beaded items. There were the flaws, as obvious as could be. Then I borrowed a little round quilted pillow from one of my neighbors. It, too, had a flaw.

When the Cub Scouts came to my house the next day, five of them wanted to know why I had "wrecked" their ornaments; the sixth one, Mike, was strutting around telling everyone how wonderful his looked.

I sat them down around the kitchen table and told them about the Native Americans putting a flaw in their beadwork, and I showed them photos in the library book. I also showed them the flaw in the little round quilted pillow I had borrowed from a neighbor. Then I gave them their ornaments and sent them all home.

About twenty-five minutes later, Pat and Mike's mom called and said, "Rita, every once in a while I need an explanation about what goes on at these den meetings. This is one of those times. Can you please explain to me why Pat is grinning from ear to ear over his little white snowman with the green blob across its belly, and Mike is in his bedroom crying, 'Mine's too perfect! Mine's too perfect!'"

I cherish this story and hold it close to my heart, because for me it was the turning point in really grasping the difference between excellence and perfection . . . and the first step toward conquering my procrastination problem. I believe it is truly liberating (and can help preserve your sanity) to cultivate an attitude of "striving for excellence but not perfection."

FEAR OF THE UNKNOWN

This fear is probably the most common. Sometimes the known circumstances are horrible, painful, and frightening, but still they are more comfortable to handle than the terrors of the unknown. Some people put off leaving abusive relationships or destructive, negative jobs because they'd rather endure the misery of "what is" than face the terror of "what might be." Lindsay loves being a veterinarian but hates the animal hospital where she has worked for the past two years because she and the boss just don't get along. Lindsay believes that she would receive better pay and feel more appreciated anywhere else, plus she commutes over an hour each way in nerve-racking traffic. Still, Lindsay doesn't do anything to find a new place to work. She procrastinates because she finds some kind of comfort in staying where she is so unhappy.

Fear of Judgment

Are you the kind of person who frequently thinks, "What will the neighbors say?" or "What will people think?" If so, you may find yourself immobilized by the fear of judgment. Many people will postpone worthy goals indefinitely simply because they don't want to run the risk of feeling embarrassed or being labeled lazy, stupid, foolish, or idealistic.

Fear of Making Mistakes

This fear inhibits many people. They don't realize that mistakes can teach us important lessons—both big and little. Jill described how years ago she became aware that every time she broke something in the kitchen—a coffee mug, a plate—it was because she was trying to do too much too quickly.

One day Jill was racing to get everything done, and just as she was ready to leave the house, she accidentally smashed a glass on the floor. It occurred to her that if that broken glass hadn't reminded her to shift gears and slow down, her high-speed pace could have led her to a traffic ticket or, worse, an auto accident.

I've often told my kids—by words and by example— that when mistakes happen, rather than beat yourself up, look at them as an inevitable part of life and ask yourself, "What can I learn from this?"

When my son, Robb, was five years old, he loved peanut butter and jelly on warm toast. One day we were involved in a project upstairs, and lunchtime came along. Robb said, "Don't worry, Mom, I'll make lunch." A few minutes later, a wonderful smell wafted up the stairs. I went downstairs to find Robb on the kitchen counter with the most bewildered look on his face, staring into the toaster, which now was billowing black smoke. He had put the peanut butter and jelly on the bread before popping it into the toaster. He looked perplexed, and said, "I don't know what to learn from this mistake. What other way is there to do it?"

> ❧
>
> The person who never makes a mistake
> probably isn't doing anything.
>
> ❧

And that's the question to ask when you fail, make a mistake, or feel foolish. Don't berate yourself. Instead of beating yourself up asking, "Why am I so dumb or such a loser?" ask "What other way is there to do it?"

Mistakes teach us that there has to be another way to do something. Supposedly, Thomas Edison had 1,600 experiments fail before he invented the lightbulb. When a friend asked him why he was wasting so much time on the project when he wasn't accomplishing anything, Edison replied, "Of course I'm accomplishing something. I've learned 1,600 ways it doesn't work!"

Yet so many procrastinators have such an overwhelming fear of making a mistake, such a terror of not being able to do something as well as they think they should or might like to, that they choose to do nothing at all. You can allow the possibility of mistakes to turn you into a timid procrastinator, or you can defuse your fear by accepting mistakes as glitches in your plans. These glitches point out when it's time to change course or change pace or find a new direction or change your mind.

Fear of Success

This fear is one of the more subtle causes of procrastination. Some people believe (whether consciously or subconsciously) that success has negative connotations. They think success must mean you are self-serving, shallow, materialistic, snobbish, and so on. Others believe succeeding sets up expectations that you must continue to succeed more and more—or must succeed at everything you do.

If you suspect that by procrastinating you are "sabotaging" your success, ask yourself, "What would happen if . . . ?" Keep repeating the question until you arrive at the core of the problem. Consider the following conversation I had with a coworker who was writing what I considered to be a terrific mystery novel. She had stopped writing, and although she claimed that she wanted with all her heart to finish the book, she had not written one word in two and a half years.

"What would happen if you started writing again?" I asked.

"Well, I'd probably finish the book."

"And what would happen if you finished the book?"

"I'd probably get it published. Everybody tells me it's great."

"What would happen if it were published?"

"I think it might be a best-seller."

"What would happen if it were a best-seller?"

"I'd probably make a lot more money than I'm making now."

"What would happen if you were making a lot more money?"

"Hmm—well—um, I think the only reason I'm staying married is because I can't support myself and the kids on my pay. If I were making a lot more money . . ."

At that point, she realized she had a lot of soul-searching to do. Did she really want a divorce? Was she remaining in the marriage only because she needed her husband's financial support? Or did she want to work on saving her marriage? Once she recognized the root of her fear and came up with answers to some important questions, she was able to return to writing her novel.

Fear of Having to Live Up to a High Standard

A variation on the fear of success, this fear can kick in when you try something new and are extremely successful at it. That is what happened to Patricia's son, Connor. He had always been an average student, but when he received his first report card in seventh grade, he was surprised that he had made the honor roll for the first time. He handed over his report card, not with a smile but with a worried, concerned look. He said, "Please don't expect me to do this again."

This fear affects adults as well as children. Is it keeping you from putting forth your best effort?

Fear of Change

Fear of change is a natural apprehension taken to an extreme. Change is one of the major causes of stress, and for many of us, it feels as if change is occurring almost daily in every aspect of our lives. Almost nobody likes change, so some people will put off moving forward in life with hopes that they can avoid the dread of change.

Curt is a case in point. He worked in a factory, loved computers, and had finally started taking computer courses in the evenings. He wanted to move into a computer job, but he kept procrastinating when it was time to write his résumé and follow through on job leads. He worried that he would be working in a stuffy office where his coworkers were snobs in three-piece suits and would put down his love of bowling.

After recognizing and confronting his fears, Curt began his job search and landed a new computer job, which he loves. He has remained close to his old friends, likes his new coworkers, still loves to bowl, and best of all, does not have to wear a suit to work. Identifying his fears gave him the courage to go ahead with his plans.

FEAR OF TOO MUCH RESPONSIBILITY

This fear keeps people from pushing themselves to do their best. Both Rachel and Steve are afraid of taking on too much responsibility. Rachel has been talking about starting a newsletter for her professional association for over three years. She worries that once she publishes the first issue, she won't be able to keep up with putting together a newsletter on a regular basis, so she does nothing.

Steve speaks often of wanting to become a Little League coach, but he has so many concerns. "What if I won't get any help from the parents? What if the kids will be too much for me to handle?" He won't know the answers until he tries coaching, but he just keeps putting it off. In the meantime, he is losing the chance to have a positive experience with his daughter, and the kids are missing out on the talents of a terrific, fun-loving man.

Fear of Feelings

When you suffer from this fear, you procrastinate, not because of how you feel *now*, but because of how you *may* feel if you take a particular action. You want to avoid feeling angry or guilty or experiencing another unpleasant emotion.

Marion, for example, has been having problems with her roommate, Nancy. She has decided to broach the subject with Nancy, but she never finds the right time to do it. Meanwhile, her stomach has been upset for weeks because she's procrastinating rather than risking an angry confrontation with Nancy.

Like Marion, Tim doesn't want to risk unleashing powerful feelings. He'd rather struggle to meet business expenses than confront his delinquent customers because he's afraid he'll feel guilty or cruel if he calls them and asks for the money he is owed.

When you put off something because you fear the feelings that might result, consider what feelings you're going through now due to your procrastination. As we discussed in chapter 1, it takes more of an emotional toll on you to put off something you dread than to go ahead and perform the task.

Fear of Finishing

Some people are afraid that as soon as they finish what they're working on, there will just be another crummy job to do. They reason that they may as well drag out this one as long as they possibly can.

Rory came up against this fear when he was redecorating his bedroom. He stripped the old wallpaper off the walls, then went out and bought some beautiful new paper. Four months later, his bedroom was still torn apart and the job was only half done. It wouldn't have taken him long to complete the job, but subconsciously, he dreaded finishing because he didn't want to start the next project.

Sometimes people fear finishing a job when it has become comfortable or has added a sense of meaning or purpose to their lives. When a project must end, but you hate to see it end, it's pretty easy to start dragging your feet. Carol, a municipal clerk, remembers a time when she was compiling a service directory for the village she served. She realizes now that she loved contacting all the service providers and finding out about their services so she could write up a summary in the directory. Carol's enthusiasm for the project energized her, and she hated to see it end. So she started (not consciously, of course) to procrastinate and slow down her progress. Once she realized what she was doing, she set a goal to wrap up the directory as soon as possible. If she caught herself slowing down, she came up with a reward (such as lunch out with friends) as each section was completed. Now that she recognizes the problems that can result from the fear of finishing, Carol passes on this information every time she presents an orientation for new employees.

Fear of finishing also occurs when there is a concern that the completed project will be unsuccessful or disappointing. Kevin has been building a boat in his basement for years. Friends needle him that once it's finished, it will be too big to fit through the doorway. But in spite of the ribbing, Kevin just can't push himself to get back to working on that boat. Maybe he's not afraid of finishing it; maybe he's just lost his enthusiasm. Maybe he doesn't want a homemade boat anymore, in which case, it's time to abandon ship (pun intended) and figure out how to get rid of it. On the other hand, if he's procrastinating because he is afraid the boat won't meet his expectations, he should consider whether he may be a perfectionist. An attitude adjustment may be needed. Either way, Kevin must realize he has a choice; then he can decide whether to finish the boat or get rid of it.

In most cases, after we choose to do a project, we also have the power to choose to end it.

FEAR OF BEING REJECTED

We are all touched by the fear of being rejected. We tend to take rejection personally, as proof that we are flawed, or imperfect. Yet each of us is flawed in one way or another.

When someone says no to our sales pitch or invitation, we don't hear it as "No, I don't want to buy your product" or "No, I'm not able to go out with you Saturday." Instead, we hear it as "No, I don't want anything to do with you,

you miserable worthless worm." Craig, who sells contracts for a professional staffing service, used to do anything to avoid making phone calls because he never knew what to say to himself when people rejected his proposals. Now he keeps a sign near the phone with the word *next* written in giant letters, and every time someone says no to him, he has developed the habit of saying "next" and reaching to dial the next number.

With our self-talk, we can stop putting off tasks, decisions, and relationships just because we are terrified that somehow, someone will judge us as flawed.

FEAR OF MAKING THE WRONG DECISION

Have you ever heard someone—maybe even yourself—say with regret, "I still haven't gotten around to replacing that old whatchamacallit . . . or changing jobs . . . or losing weight . . . or looking up my old friend . . . or quitting smoking . . . or whatever"? The problem, frequently, is not the replacing or changing or looking up; it's the *deciding* to do it.

Making decisions drives some people crazy. Once the decision is made, they can function fine; they go ahead and do what they have to do. But when it's time to decide to do something, they become busy with a million other things that just push that decision right out of their minds. Making decisions brings many people to a crashing standstill. I've often thought that some bright entrepreneur could become a millionaire by opening up a decision-making business. "Step right up, folks. Tell me the decision you need to make, pay me a small fortune, and tell ya what I'm gonna do. I'll decide for you."

Some of us would love to have another person take over all our decision making, but sadly, most of our decisions cannot be made by anyone other than ourselves.

If we're terrified of making the wrong decision, we put off doing anything until we're sure the decision we make will be 100 percent correct.

When people are stuck in a decision-making situation and can't make up their minds about something, they tend to feel agitated and frustrated. During a Conquer Procrastination discussion, Josephine said, "I'd rather make the wrong decision than hang undecided. When I'm undecided about something, it seems to consume my thoughts and I can't think of anything else."

Another participant, Tony, told the group: "When my procrastination was at its peak, I would go the opposite way. I'd put the decision out of my mind and say, 'I'll try to decide later.' Now I follow the wise advice my favorite philosopher, Yoda, gave in the film *The Empire Strikes Back*: 'Do or do not. There is no try.' I used to have knots in my stomach when I was indecisive, especially when I was trying to fall asleep. Now the knots are gone; right or wrong, decisions are handled immediately, not left till later."

Maybe you don't fear making the wrong decision so much as you hate having to live with the results. Well, not all decisions are carved in stone. Granted, some are, but most choices you make are reversible, especially if you make the decision while keeping in mind that someday you might want the option to change it.

Kortenay procrastinated about buying a new sofa. She had been living with an old hand-me-down sofa for the five years she had been married. She and her husband had saved for a new one, she had shopped around quite a bit, and she had selected the style, the fabric, and color of a custom sofa. All she had to do was place the order. Eight months went by. But no amount of urging or encouraging could budge her. Something about ordering this custom sofa struck a chord of terror deep within her.

After talking with her awhile, I realized that Kortenay had very little experience buying furniture, and some of her choices seemed, to her, to be disastrous. Her husband left all the decisions to her, yet he had been unhappy with and critical of several of her purchases.

Custom furniture might be fine for others, and might be great for Kortenay after she has gained more experience and confidence in this area, but at this time in her life, she'd do better buying from a store with a solid return policy. Once she realized this, she stopped procrastinating. She found a sofa, which was similar to what she had planned to order, and had it delivered. After a week, she discovered that both she and her husband hated it. They returned the sofa, bought another in a different color and slightly different design, and have been very happy with it.

Like Kortenay, Ken was afraid of making the wrong decision. In his case, he wanted to invest in a mutual fund but was afraid he'd pick the wrong one. So he did nothing—for years. Finally, he figured out how to overcome his inertia. When considering a mutual fund, he started to key in on how much it would cost him to liquidate the fund. If there was a percent penalty, he computed the exact cost. Then he decided on what he considered to be a wise investment, knowing that if circumstances changed, he could withdraw his money for a fairly low fee.

Alberto's procrastinating had to do with selecting some promotional products that would advertise his two health clubs. He talked with distributors, looked through dozens of catalogs, and viewed hundreds of advertising specialty items at a "promotional expo." But Alberto feared making an expensive mistake and being stuck with thousands of useless giveaways if he made the wrong decision, so he procrastinated for months. Eventually Alberto, decided to order only 300 key chains and pass up the chance to place an order of 2,000, which had a much lower cost per item. In a month, he knew the product wasn't as popular as he'd hoped, but that knowledge moved him in the right direction. Now he gives out a small flashlight key chain that his customers love and value enough to carry with them, which is exactly the kind of advertising that Mike was hoping for.

If you are procrastinating over a decision because it is (or appears to be) irreversible, see if there's a way to take the pressure off yourself. Maybe there's a return policy or a cancellation clause; perhaps you can put a short-term time limit on your commitment, order a smaller quantity, or somehow work out a way to "change course" if the decision doesn't pan out.

Using Research and Consultants to Help with Decision Making

Sometimes people dread making a decision because they don't have enough information. They feel stupid, inadequate, or ignorant. They know they should see a doctor but don't know how to select the right one. Or they don't know how to find the right lawyer, contractor, financial adviser or repair technician. Or they wish they could forever put off decisions on buying a car or whatever it is they need. They believe others know the right way to make this purchase, but they lack the expertise.

The solution to this dilemma is to do research or find a consultant. Let's take these one at a time. By research, I don't mean spending hours poring over statistics; I mean talking to friends or others who own or have bought what you want to buy, or who deal with the profession you need to work with. You'd be surprised at how glad (and flattered) people are to offer help and advice.

People who sell the product can be of great help with your research. If you're shopping for a computer, for example, go to three different stores and ask someone in each store to spend some time explaining the features of various computers to you. If the salespeople pressure you to buy, tell them the truth; you are comparison shopping, you have a few more stops to make, but you might be back. By the time you leave the third store, you'll have a list of intelligent questions to ask, you'll have a good idea of what you like and don't like, and you'll feel that you are an informed person who, whether you decide to continue to shop around or return to one of the three stores, can make a wise decision.

It's the same if you are having some work done on your home or at the office. Set up appointments with representatives from three different companies to come out and give you a free estimate. If any of them push you to sign a contract, say that you're comparing prices, you'll be seeing a few more people, but you might end up using his or her firm. Again, you'll wind up with a list of intelligent questions and a lot of knowledge about the subject (and perhaps even a better price).

Sometimes, when you research a "dream" or a solution to a problem, you'll be surprised at how affordable it is. Gisela hated the ugly green, old-fashioned counter in her kitchen, but she thought it would cost thousands to remodel it. After shopping around, she installed (with the help of her brother) a beautiful new countertop for less than the cost of an inexpensive TV she had bought for the kitchen the previous year. You learn a lot from this type of research, and you may be astounded to discover that you actually enjoy doing it.

Now, what about consultants? I don't mean that you should pay a fortune to some consulting firm; instead call someone you know who works in the field or has a lot of knowledge in your area of interest. Ask that individual to spend some time with you explaining what to look for or giving you some recommendations, or, better yet, ask him or her to come along with you when you go shopping. If you feel awkward about asking, offer to treat your consultant to lunch, or to provide a favor in return, or to somehow find some fair compensation.

Peggy needed to buy a new car but hated to shop for one because she knew absolutely nothing about automobiles. I suggested that she find a consultant, a friend who knew about and loved cars, and ask that person to come along on a shopping trip. She had a male friend who fit the bill, but she was reluctant to ask him because she thought it would make her look stupid.

I don't agree. Nobody can know everything about everything. We are all ignorant in some areas. That doesn't mean we're stupid; it just means we don't know a lot about a certain subject. To me, asking for advice from someone who has expertise in an area in which I am ignorant is an intelligent move that will lead to wise decision making.

Eileen, a campground owner, wasn't shy about using a consultant. In fact, she used several. She knew she needed to upgrade her software to help make running her business easier, but she kept putting it off and struggling with the old, inadequate programs. She didn't know exactly what she needed, so finally she started asking around and several of her friends gave her advice to help her decide what would be best for her needs. One friend went with her to the computer store, they had a fun day exploring the latest in software, and thanks to her consultants, Eileen wound up with new software that had all the features she needed.

The more thought you give to and the more experience you acquire in making decisions, the more confident you will feel as a decision maker. As your confidence increases, your dread and fear of decisions will decrease. There may be times when you feel "burned out" from making decisions; then you need to take a break from decision making for a while. But that's a conscious decision and is different from procrastinating or avoiding decisions because you fear or dread them.

Prioritizing Decisions

Sometimes you'll need to prioritize decisions, either because you have too many to make, and you can't possibly tackle them all at once, or because you don't want to spend $1,000 worth of energy and effort on a $10 decision or vice versa.

For example, Therese spent weeks shopping for a $300 VCR but plopped down $2,000 on some investments to which she had given very little thought or time. The larger or more costly the weight of the decision, the more thought and energy it deserves. Therese needs to work on prioritizing when it comes to decision making.

The Consequences of
Not Making a Decision

It is said that not to decide is itself a decision. That's true, and it can be a big mistake.

People think that putting off decisions makes their lives easier. So they pay a fortune repairing the old clunker of a car because they absolutely hate the decisions involved in buying a new or used car. They live with patched or semirepaired items that never quite work, not because they can't afford replacements but because they never make up their minds to go shopping. They dream for years of a vacation, but they never start saving money or planning for it. They continue smoking, abusing alcohol or drugs, gambling, being overweight, or staying in an abusive relationship because they never decide to seek counseling or to use other help available to them.

Then, when they reach old age, they regret that they never improved their skills or followed their dream to build a better life for themselves or their families. They wonder what went wrong, never realizing that their lack of decision making would eventually catch up with them. Most people don't spend a lot of time regretting their wrong decisions; the deep regrets are usually for the decisions they never made.

How Do I Conquer a Fear?

There are way too many fears to cover them all in this chapter. Nevertheless, I can give some advice that will help you conquer most fears that are causing you to procrastinate. You need to ask yourself two questions—and then answer them honestly.

First, ask yourself, "What am I afraid of?" Simply identifying the fear—giving it a name—often takes away the power it holds over you.

The second question to ask is: "What if my worst fear came true in the most horrible way possible?" Let's say someone rejects you by declaring, "No, I wouldn't buy your product if my life depended on it." You'd be hurt, sure, but would you survive? Of course you would. What if you do make a mistake, or look stupid, or make the wrong decision? You've done it before, and you'll do it again. It's a miserable feeling, but it won't kill you. Whatever your fear, magnify that fear as much as possible. Think of the worst thing that could happen. You would survive it, wouldn't you? Sometimes, the worst thing that could happen isn't nearly as bad as how miserable you feel being a procrastinator.

Once you identify your fear and face it, once you magnify that fear and decide you'll survive it and perhaps even learn from it, you can start moving and do whatever it is you've been putting off—and start taking control of your life.

ॐ

THOUGHTS TO CONSIDER

Perfectionism is NOT a quest for the best. It is a pursuit of the worst in ourselves, the part that tells us that nothing we do will ever be good enough—that we should try again.

—Julia Cameron

A man would do nothing if he waited until he could do it so well that no one could find fault with it.

—Unknown

When you aim for perfection you discover it's a moving target.

—George Fisher

There is no perfect time to write. There's only now.

—Barbara Kingsolver

ॐ

THOUGHTS FOR CONQUERING FEARS

We should not let our fears hold us back from pursuing our hopes.

—John F. Kennedy

What you are afraid to do is a clear indication of the next thing you need to do.

—Ralph Waldo Emerson

FEAR is spelled
False
Expectations
Appearing
Real

—Unknown

ତ୍ତ

THOUGHTS ABOUT DECISION MAKING

Security is mostly a superstition. It does not exist in nature. Life is either a daring adventure or nothing.

—Helen Keller

Though right or wrong you're bound to find
Relief in making up your mind.

—Thornton Burgess

In any moment of decision,
the very best thing you can do, is what is right;
the next best thing you can do, is what is wrong;
the worst thing you can do is NOTHING.

—Teddy Roosevelt

EXTRA CREDIT

1. In the left-hand column, list the top five things you are putting off at this time in your life.

————————————— —————————————
————————————— —————————————
————————————— —————————————
————————————— —————————————
————————————— —————————————

2. In the right-hand column, opposite each, list the fear that is holding you back.

3. What fears, in general, seem to cause you to procrastinate? Write them down. ————————————

—————————————————————————————
—————————————————————————————

4. Refer to your list of "101 Things You've Been Putting Off," selecting the ten things you most want to do.

   • Are they different from the top five you just wrote?
   • What part does perfectionism play in putting them off? Have you been waiting for the perfect time or circumstances?

If I Had My Life to Live Over Again

By Nadine Stair of Louisville, Kentucky,
who was eighty-five years old when she wrote this

I'd dare to make more mistakes next time. I'd relax. I would limber up. I would be sillier than I have been this trip. I would take fewer things seriously. I would take more chances. I would take more trips. I would climb more mountains and swim more rivers. I would eat more ice cream and less beans. I would perhaps have more actual troubles, but I'd have fewer imaginary ones.

You see, I'm one of those people who live sensibly and sanely hour after hour, day after day. Oh, I've had my moments, and if I had it to do over again, I'd have more of them. In fact, I'd try to have nothing else. Just moments. One after another, instead of living so many years ahead of each day. I've been one of those people who never go anywhere without a thermometer, a hot water bottle, a raincoat, and a parachute. If I had it to do again, I would travel lighter next time.

If I had my life to live over, I would start barefoot earlier in the spring and stay that way later in the fall. I would go to more dances. I would ride more merry-go-rounds. I would pick more daisies.

5

"I Wanna Do It All"

IRONICALLY, ONE OF THE reasons people put off doing things is that they want to do everything. And they want to do it all at once. They want the impossible.

Some I-Wanna-Do-It-All Procrastinators are highly energetic and ambitious, although not necessarily driven by money. Some are on the fast track. Some are struggling to survive after a "downsizing" and are doing the work of two or three people. But the pressure and frantic feeling doesn't end when the I-Wanna-Do-It-All people leave work. They have a ton of things to do at home and a briefcase packed with papers.

But they have no time for family.

No time for friends.

No time for fun.

No time for a life.

I heard a cute story about a first grader who asked her father why Mommy brings so much work from the office to do at home. He explained that Mommy can't get it finished during her workday. The six-year-old asked, "Well, why don't they just move her to a slower group?"

Maybe that option doesn't exist, but it's worth asking why we are all so busy. Is it possible that being busy is the new status symbol of our age? ("You think *you're* busy; let me tell you about everything *I'm* involved in.") Have you ever received one of those Christmas letters from a family listing all the activities of the kids, followed by paragraphs about the parents that begin, "He's a busy guy, too . . ."and "She sure is keeping busy . . ."? It's almost as if being busy equals being successful: "Let me tell you how busy I am so you'll know how very, very well I'm doing."

ARE YOU A SANE PROCRASTINATOR?

Some people put off starting or completing tasks because they are constantly drawn to new activities. They possess a combination of what I call Super Attention and Natural

Enthusiasm (SANE). This type of procrastinator becomes totally engrossed in an interesting project and then halfway through it is lured away by something even more exciting.

Dottie, the president of a successful business, practices this type of procrastination. "Since I was a kid, I've had this weird souped-up attention," she says. "It would snap into gear, and I would zero in on something that interested me, become very enthusiastic about it, and not think of or hear or notice anything else. If a teacher caught my attention, I couldn't tear myself away. If I'm reading a terrific book, nothing else in the world exists. But then, something else would grab me and take over my full, undivided, super attention and I'd forget about the first thing. The result was procrastination."

Super Attention can take control of your life. You have too many projects going at once (none finished) because halfway through one amazingly interesting idea, another comes along that is even more interesting. Your calendar is packed with dates, meetings, get-togethers, parties, and classes. You're usually reading more than one book at a time. You may have the TV and radio going while you work. In conversations, you tend to jump quickly from one topic to another, never finishing any of them. This behavior pattern results in a life of excitement, exhilaration . . . and exhaustion.

Ironically, many overachievers seem to display signs of having Super Attention and Natural Enthusiasm, and because their attention bounces from one thing to another, they leave lots of projects and plans unfinished. If you re-

Four Signs That You're a Sane Procrastinator

1. When you're engrossed in what you're doing, you become oblivious to what's going on around you.
2. While you are in the middle of one project, you reach for the phone or start another.
3. Your interest in activities is fleeting. For example, you're excited about planting vegetables in your garden; then by harvest time, the thrill is gone, so you leave everything to rot on the vine. Or you have many unfinished craft and hobby projects around the house (or sports equipment and musical instruments that are never used).
4. Your desk or dining room table is covered with clutter, but you know exactly how to find everything in all the stacks, piles, and boxes.

late to this, you don't have to stifle your curiosity or enthusiasm for new things in order to complete the project you've started. For example, set a timer to focus your efforts on the present task. Or when you think of a new project or idea while you're working on something else, let starting the new project be your reward for completing the present one. Using these and other anticrastination strategies in this book, you'll learn to stick with a task or to keep track of—and return to—projects instead of abandoning them when something else captures your attention.

TIME TO TALK TO YOURSELF

If you're an I-Wanna-Do-It-All Procrastinator, one effective solution is to start talking to yourself, though not necessarily out loud. Every time you shift into high gear, tell yourself you can't do everything. It's time to be selective. Time to delegate. Time to eliminate. Time to streamline. Time to choose your battles. Time to prioritize. Tell yourself, "This is important to finish. The other stuff will have to be put on the back burner."

When my kids were young, I was a stay-at-home mom, and like most other families living on one paycheck, we had very little money. I would become so anxious and worried when we didn't have enough money to pay bills that I was making myself sick. Then, when our financial situation was at its worst, I came across the poem "Hyacinths to Feed Thy Soul" (see box on page 104), which helped me regain my balance. That poem became part of my philosophy of life, and when our bills stretched beyond our cash, I'd seek out "free day" at the zoo or museum, or I'd pack a picnic lunch and explain to my kids that even when we're broke, we must always remember to have hyacinths to feed our souls.

As the years went by, I came to realize that time—to me—had become as scarce and as precious as money. On those days when I felt like a hamster running in a wheel, when there was no time to pause or plan or take a break— those were exactly the times when I had to jump off the wheel and pause to connect with my family or just take a break. My kids really understood this concept, because when things at home would start speeding by at a frantic pace, one of them would say, "Time for hyacinths to feed the soul," and we'd all step off the hamster wheel and become human again.

HYACINTHS TO FEED THY SOUL

by Gulistan Saadi
If of thy mortal goods thou art bereft,
And from thy slender store
Two loaves alone to thee are left,
Sell one, and with the dole
Buy hyacinths to feed thy soul.

As our family expanded, we passed along this philosophy. Back in 1994, my son, Robb, married a wonderful young woman named Michelle. One week before their wedding, Robb, Michelle, and I were walking along a lake with a picnic basket. It was a glorious October day—brilliant blue sky, scarlet and golden trees, crisp autumn air— and the soon-to-be bride, looking down at her feet as we walked, was muttering, "I've got six days left till the wedding. I have so many lists of things to do that I have a giant list listing all the lists, and here I am going on a picnic and Robb says you're going to explain why we're doing this and it has to do with hyacinths."

I laughed and told her about the poem and what it meant to me, and we continued on with our picnic. It was a truly refreshing, "re-creating" afternoon, and Michelle said that when she returned to the countdown of the last few days preparing for the wedding, she felt much more centered and balanced; much more focused on the wedding being about their marriage rather than about response cards, the banquet hall, and all the other details.

In 1996, Robb and Michelle became the parents of a baby boy named Connor Patrick Emmett. When Connor was three months old, Michelle—besides being immersed in new-baby activities—was studying for her board exams for nursing school. She phoned me asking if I wanted to join her and Connor for a picnic lunch at the park. I said, "But, Michelle, you're so busy with your studying and the baby and everything."

"I know," she replied. "We're taking a break, and it has to do with hyacinths."

She "got" it! And I hope you get it, too. When you are feeling swamped and overwhelmed with too much to do, that's when it's time to pause, jump off that hamster wheel, and re-create yourself.

Dolores, a comptroller who is doing the work of several people and leads a frantically busy life, tells herself, "I have a life expectancy of seventy-eight years. This activity will have to be put off for now, but I hope someday I'll have time to join that group, learn that skill, or start that project." By talking to herself in this way, she retains her sanity and smooths out some of the stress in her life. It's OK to want to do it all—as long as you remind yourself you can't do everything at once. You must learn to say no once in a while.

In many instances, you procrastinate because you are overwhelmed. You are too busy, too overbooked. If you're an I-Wanna-Do-It-All Procrastinator, you love life, and love to live it to the fullest. Every idea that comes up is appealing. Every cause seems worthy. Every activity sounds great. Every person needs you. So you say yes to everything, then juggle too many commitments . . . and procrastinate.

THE POWER OF SETTING LIMITS

The first step in breaking the cycle is to set limits. When asked to do more than you can handle, reply, "I'd love to give my time to this worthy cause, but I can't right now." Or "I'd love to attend this social gathering, but I can't this month."

Some people find that they don't need to eliminate activities in their lives, but they do benefit from scheduling "just say no" days on their calendars. They block out a certain day (or portion of a day) to catch up on things. Then they decline any invitations or activities that come up that might interfere with this blocked-out time.

Some people use these days to catch up on the many little chores they've been putting off around the house. Others use this time for planning, reevaluating, goal setting. Still others use it to relax and prevent burnout.

Most people who keep enormously busy schedules, yet still manage their time well and don't procrastinate, have learned to pace themselves. Either they take breaks during the day, or they block out time weekly, or they schedule time to connect with people or to unwind or do whatever it takes to recharge their batteries.

Burnout results from:

• not pacing yourself
• not striving for balance in your life
• not saying no when you need to.

Maria likes to set aside an occasional morning or afternoon just to catch up on things, a period of time with absolutely nothing scheduled. She'll look around the house or her desk or at her list, or sit at her computer, and do what needs to be done. Her favorite is the day after Christmas. She always sets it aside simply to recharge her battery. Knowing that day is coming up gives Maria enormous energy when she is getting ready for the holiday. She'll think to herself, "Even though I'm tired now, I can do this tonight because I've got my whole day off coming up."

If you "Wanna Do It All," you may find it very difficult to say no to activities at first or to clear some time for yourself, but with practice, it gets easier and easier. And the more comfortable you become with saying no, the more control you have over your time and your life . . . and the less you procrastinate.

I remember a particular lesson my daughter, Kerry, learned about the value of saying no. One night, after presenting an eight-hour Time Management seminar, I came home to find Kerry sitting at the table with a list in front of her. She had just started high school and had joined several school activities. She was discouraged, because in the process of wanting to do everything, she found she didn't have time to do anything, so she had written a list of all the groups she belonged to.

"Mom, I'm just swamped. I have to quit something."

Filled with enthusiasm from the seminar I had just completed, I told her, "Kerry, this is terrific! You've just discovered one of the key secrets of time management. Most people don't realize that lots of times—when their lives get too busy—they have a choice. They can choose to say no to some of their activities." My son, Robb, who had wandered into the room, looked surprised.

"Hey, Mom, is that really a secret to time management?"

"Yep."

"The secret is that when people are too busy they have a choice? They can say no to some activities?"

"Yep."

"Do you tell them that at your seminars?"

"Yep."

"Well . . . why does it take you *eight hours* to tell them that?"

THOUGHTS TO CONSIDER

If you can spend a perfectly useless afternoon in a perfectly useless manner, you have learned how to live.

—Lin Yutang

Lord, help me to sort out what I should do first, second and third today and to not try to do everything at once and nothing well. Give me the wisdom to delegate what I can and to order the things I can't delegate, to say no when I need to, and the sense to know when to go home.

—*Marion Wright Edelman*

It's easy to say "no" when there's a deeper "yes!" burning inside.

—*Unknown*

I can sit by a lake for an hour and do nothing. It's like a dream time for me. It organizes my soul.

—*Diane Sawyer*

Time is the stuff of which life is made.

—*Benjamin Franklin*

If my time is spent
Racing around
Constantly doing something,
I need some time off
Lying around
To catch up on doing nothing

—*Rita Emmett*

Sometimes you must slow down to go faster.

—*Ann McGee Cooper*

EXTRA CREDIT

If you had all the time in the world, and nothing or no one making any demands on your time,

- What would you do first? _____

_____

- What next? _____

_____

- And after that? _____

_____

- How would you feel about these accomplishments?

_____

_____

EXTRA, EXTRA CREDIT

(and now . . . a pop quiz)

1. Do I put off things important to my life because other people's priorities always come first?

$$\text{YES} \quad \text{NO}$$

2. Do I commit to so many things that there's not enough time to do any of them and I always feel overwhelmed?

$$\text{YES} \quad \text{NO}$$

3. Do I think I don't need to do all the things others need to do to manage their time?

$$\text{YES} \quad \text{NO}$$

4. Do I inconvenience my family and loved ones because I'm overbooked?

$$\text{YES} \quad \text{NO}$$

5. Do I put off taking care of tasks important to my finances, relationships, health, or career while I'm out doing other, less important things?

$$\text{YES} \quad \text{NO}$$

6. Do I say yes to so many "fun" events that they overwhelm me and are no longer fun?

$$\text{YES} \quad \text{NO}$$

7. Do I often feel fragmented, frantic, or frazzled because I'm overbooked?

$$\text{YES} \quad \text{NO}$$

8. Am I so afraid of missing out on something that I say "yes" to everything?

YES   NO

9. Do I spend time with people or groups that I used to love to be with but now no longer enjoy?

YES   NO

If you answered yes to any of these questions, part of your procrastination problem is that you need to start saying no to some requests.

6

"Help! I'm Overwhelmed"

❦

ONE OF THE PRIME REASONS people procrastinate is that they are overwhelmed . . . deluged . . . swamped. They feel flattened by the steamroller of life's things-to-do. They may have too many chores or one project that seems so huge or so complicated that they become immobilized. They stop thinking, stop deciding, stop doing anything.

Students feel swamped when they have to study for exams or when several papers are all due at the same time. At work, a person might feel deluged when launching a project or preparing for an important meeting. People in sales look at their quota and wonder, "How can I do everything it takes to reach that goal?"

At home, the overwhelming job might be sorting through paper clutter or simply keeping up with family and friends. For many people, the idea of moving to a new house or making it through the holidays is too much to deal with. Or the overwhelming job might be seasonal, such as preparing to file tax returns, or there might simply be a large number of everyday chores. Whatever the task, when we feel overwhelmed, we often become paralyzed and do nothing.

Indeed, the job may truly be overwhelming right now. There's a chance that no one has the time or energy to do the whole project that looms before you. The secret to dealing with this problem is contained in this Chinese proverb: "A journey of 10,000 miles begins with but a single step." You can find the time and energy to take a single step. But before doing so, you need to take some time to determine exactly where you want to go on your journey and the steps necessary to move you along.

If you were really taking a journey of 10,000 miles, you would want to know the destination, you'd need a map so you could plan your route, and you would need to know the method of travel. And as you planned your journey, you'd realize that it was composed of minijourneys. The first day, you'd plan to travel from point A to B, the next day from B to C, and so forth.

Break the Job into Manageable Pieces

Make a list of minijourneys by writing down all the little jobs that are part of your overwhelming project. If your list is too intimidating, break it down into several lists. Or if you have notes on little scraps of paper all over your desk, consolidate them on one sheet.

Try grouping lists chronologically. What has to be accomplished this week, next week, then the next? Can you do any prioritizing at this point? Not everything is an "A"; some things must be "C's." Or make different lists for phone calls, deskwork, research, or chasing around.

After you have identified all the little jobs that form your big project, concentrate on taking "but a single step"; focus on doing one item on your list. Then scan your list for other "single steps." If you discover that it's simply impossible for you to do each and every job, you can determine whether any job can be streamlined, delegated, or eliminated. Is there a task you could skip without compromising the project? Now you're ready to chip away at the project, one task at a time.

According to Sharon Borkowicz, a licensed real estate broker, most people think it's pretty simple for a Realtor to sell a house—just find a buyer, help the buyer get a loan, attend the closing, and you're done. So when new Realtors start in the business, they become absolutely overwhelmed with all that is involved. Sharon's office provides each staff member with a set of directions for what to do after listing a property for sale. This list includes seventy-five steps, everything from registering the property with the multiple listing service, to putting up the yard sign, to arranging for the appraisal to be done and the final walk-through. This list ensures that everything will be done, nothing will be

Twelve Tips for Working More Effectively at Your Desk

❧

1. Write down your ideas. Do not trust your memory, no matter how good it may be!
2. Set down your priorities before the start of each day's work.
3. Use your high-productivity hours for your top-priority projects.
4. Tackle time-consuming projects in stages.
5. Do not overschedule. Leave some time each day free from appointments.
6. Concentrate on one item at a time.
7. Take breaks. Walk around. Stretch. Eat lunch away from your desk.
8. Establish a place for everything. Categorize, file, and store items nearby.
9. Keep paperwork moving.
10. Put limits on visits:

    • Stack stuff on any extra chairs so uninvited visitors have to stand.

    • When chatty people call, as soon as you answer the phone tell them you have only a few minutes to talk. Politely ask them the point of their call right away.
11. Remove from your desk all papers you are not working on. This prevents lost or mixed-up papers.
12. Handle each piece of paper only once.

forgotten, and most of all, it keeps brokers from feeling overwhelmed and allows them to take one step at a time.

If your overwhelming project is something you are going to do repeatedly, don't throw away your list of minijourneys; keep it and use it over and over as they do in Sharon's office. Many business travelers frequently report that having a "list of what to bring along" has helped to eliminate that overwhelmed feeling that used to sweep over them at the thought of packing.

The Lists, the Listless, and the List Losers

"Tell me, did you call Zelda Glutznaggle and ask her about that estimate?"

"Oh gee, I'm sorry. I've been so busy . . . we're swamped at work . . . and there's so much happening in our family. I just didn't have time."

We've all heard this litany of excuses; maybe you've even mumbled them yourself. But the truth is, often you neglected the phone call (or whatever was requested) not because you were too busy but because you forgot. And why did you forget? You didn't write it down on your list of things to do. It's as simple as that.

Lists are important because they:

- help you remember to do things
- unclutter your mind
- help you take inventory
- are motivating and provide direction
- help you set goals
- help you establish priorities
- keep you focused
- are satisfying when you can cross off all your accomplishments
- help you visualize
- help organize and clarify your thinking (and can move you from generalities to specifics).

Some people who don't make lists wake up in the morning, or show up at work, and say, "I wonder what I'll do today." They wait for the phone to ring or for the boss's direction so they will know the plan for the day. They drift aimlessly from crisis to crisis. They work hard at "putting out fires" instead of preventing them. Without priorities, they spend their time doing unimportant tasks while complaining that "I have so much to do."

To be listless is an inefficient and unproductive way to live life. When you write lists, you'll find yourself spelling out specifically, exactly what you have to do.

However, the best lists won't help you if you lose them. List Losers make lists on giant pieces of paper, itty-bitty scraps of paper, crumpled envelopes, and the back of bank deposit slips. Their lists are scattered around their living area, strewn across their workplace, stuffed in their wallets and purses, and strategically placed in their cars. They religiously, zealously record everything on a list but can't remember where they put it.

Why do some folks go through life writing and losing lists? It's basically a matter of not being organized. Designate a place to put your list, then always return it there. Some people have a special spot on the refrigerator for their lists; others have a certain place in a drawer, in their wallet or purse, on their desk, in their computer—it doesn't matter where the place is, just as long as you have one specific place you can count on to put it and to find it.

৶

EMMETT'S LAW OF LOSS

If certain things in your life are always hard to find, it's probably because they don't have their own special place.

৶

I've known people with large families or busy households who find a regular hiding place for their daily to-do lists. One mother of six kids told me she slides her list between the gravy boat and the wall on the top shelf of her kitchen cabinet. That sounds rather awkward to me, but she said it has worked for her for the past fifteen years. Prior to this system, her kids were always moving or misplacing her list or using it as scrap paper.

People stash lists in Bibles, plastic storage bowls, under the portable TV, on top of the refrigerator, all kinds of odd places. If you keep an appointment calendar, you can write the list, review it, and tuck it into the calendar. The trick is to find one regular place and write and refer to your list daily. Maintaining and safeguarding your list will become a habit. Good habits are as easy to form as bad habits.

If you lose lists because you write them on small pieces of paper that are easily mislaid or discarded, the solution is simple: use bigger paper. You could use a *pad* of paper. They come in all colors, and proclaiming one as your private property may encourage others to say, "It's blue paper. Must be Maureen's list. Hands off." My husband, Bruce, uses a clipboard. It's legal size, and it's red. Looks a bit strange lying around the house (the clipboard, not the husband), but it's really hard to lose a large, red, legal-sized clipboard.

Spiral notebooks are a terrific way to conquer list losing. Certainly it's possible to lose them, but they are a lot easier to find than tiny scraps of paper. In fact, get into the habit of consolidating all your little lists and phone messages for the day onto one sheet in your notebook.

Ruth, an environmental engineer, keeps a spiral notebook in the top drawer of her desk at work. When she is greeted with a stack of those little "while you were out" phone messages to return, she copies the name and phone number onto her spiral notebook list. This avoids a lot of messy papers floating around her desk, and it eliminates that sense of chaos all those little papers seem to create.

If you choose to work with a spiral notebook, date the top of your list and don't tear out the pages once you've checked off everything on the list. There is a wonderful, exhilarating feeling when you flip back through the pages every now and then and realize all you've accomplished. Also, it's helpful when you find yourself wondering "Did I make that phone call?" to glance back over the past few pages and see that the phone call was made and checked off; plus the date at the top of the page lets you know when the call was made. (An extra bonus: If you failed to record that phone number, and needed it again, it would still be in your notebook.)

Now, what do you do when each time you make up a new list, you keep carrying over the same unfinished item or items from the old list? Well, it's time to make a decision. Either do it today, or set a date for doing it and mark it on your calendar, or decide you're never going to do it.

When you decide not to carry over an item on your list, write beside it, "Omit. Not a Priority," or "ONAP." This helps in a couple of ways. First, when you look back to see if you did it, there is no confusion. You're not wondering if it's crossed out because it's done or if you decided against it. Second, if a week or two later you're checking through your notebook lists to see whether that item was done, you won't feel guilty because you didn't do whatever it was. Reading "Omit. Not a Priority" or "ONAP" tells you that you made a definite decision, based on available time and priorities. Of course, sometimes circumstances change. If it suddenly becomes important to do the item, you can just add it again to your list, then make sure it's one of the first things you do that day.

In addition to these tips on how to keep from being a List Loser due to being disorganized, we have to look at another reason that people lose lists. Are you writing your list to humor someone (perhaps even yourself) and then losing that list as a way to rebel? Losing it because you don't want to do—and have no intention of doing—one single item on it? It's a pretty silly game to play, isn't it? Take a minute to answer this question: Whom are you hurting by losing that list?

PORTABLE PROJECT CENTER

Every once in a while, a job comes along that involves more than writing a list. If your project involves collecting cost estimates from different sources, saving receipts, or accumulating a lot of information or papers, create for yourself a Portable Project Center. Buy a folder with pockets plus a spiral notebook; both should be the same color so you can keep them together easily. Store the notebook inside the folder when you're not using it. Now every bit of information that involves your project can be either stuffed into the folder pockets or jotted into the notebook. Use different-colored Portable Project Centers for all large, overwhelming projects in your professional and your personal life.

Paddy, a homeowner, used this system for months during extensive remodeling on his house. His kids needled him about his constantly shouting, "Hey, has anyone seen my green folder and notebook?" but he claims it's the most organized he has ever been with a do-it-yourself project.

A good trick—actually an indispensable trick—is to find a safe place to keep your folder and to get into the habit of putting it there. Place every piece of data in your Portable Project Center. Write your to-do lists in the notebook with a date at the top of the page, and don't throw out the page when the list is done; just check off what's completed. Use the back pages to record important phone numbers. Don't keep little scraps of paper with phone numbers on them; they'll only (you guessed it) overwhelm you.

Tuck receipts, drawings, brochures, photos, pages torn from magazines and catalogs, charts, bids, and everything else related to your project in the pockets of the folder. But don't clutter it up with information from other projects. Buy a separate folder and notebook for those, and again, color-match them.

Now, if you have to transport project information from work to home, or from one place to another, you'll have all the information gathered in one complete portable package. As you work on your project, refer to your list frequently but take just one step at a time, one task at a time. And enjoy the satisfaction of checking off items as you complete them.

Georgia, a manager of external relations for a large corporation, uses a Portable Project Center for each of the two conferences she plans and coordinates each year. She begins with a color-coordinated pocket folder and spiral notebook and puts everything in them: the list of ideas for the theme, brochures from all potential conference sites, material for presenters at the general and breakout sessions, giveaways, publicity ideas, registration materials, name tags, and so forth. She writes all lists, phone numbers, and notes on communications in the spiral notebook and tucks receipts and everything else in the pocket folder. She loves the fact that her project is portable. The file gets tucked in her briefcase and travels with her wherever she goes. Any information she needs is always handy.

Georgia also records her to-do list in the notebook; she enjoys checking off her daily achievements, and when she feels as if she's ready to burn out, she likes to flip back through previous lists to review all she has accomplished.

Once the conference ends, Georgia files away all the material—still in the notebook, so that, in addition to the file label, the notebook's rim of color shows when she looks in her file cabinet. She says that the color is a trigger for her. After a while, all conferences tend to merge together in her memory, but when she's looking for something, she'll open the file drawer, look over the contents, and it will all come together. "Now I remember. Yellow file. Texas conference. Five years ago." Once it's filed away, Georgia starts a new Portable Project Center in a different color, and she's off and running again, ready to start on the next conference.

When Is the Best Time to Write Your List?

The best time to write your list—or to accomplish almost anything—depends on whether you are a morning or evening person.

Morning people open their eyes, get out of bed, and are immediately awake. They chatter, they sing, they tap-dance through the house. But somewhere between about 8:30 and 10:00 P.M., like little drooping petunias, they begin to wilt, close down, snuggle in. They have finished living life for that day.

Evening people also open their eyes and get out of bed, but they do not wake up right away. They need time to come alive. Some grab on to the handle of a coffee cup and follow it wherever it may lead them; others grumble, grunt, or simply sit in silence, ignoring the people or chaos surrounding them. Some hide behind the morning newspaper; others hide in the bathroom. But around 9:00 P.M., just as the little-drooping-petunia morning people are going into their slumping stupor, evening people pop open their eyes, a surge of energy courses through their bodies, and with a bright, expectant expression they shout, "Now I'm ready to live life!" Ironically, morning people and evening people usually marry each other.

Morning people are great at writing their lists first thing in the morning, and evening people aren't good at anything in the morning. Jim, a systems analyst, is an evening person, so the last thing he does before leaving work is make his list for the following day. Then when he arrives at work each morning, his list helps to get him aimed in the right direction. It doesn't matter whether you are a morning or evening person; when it comes to writing lists—or accomplishing just about anything— follow your inner timetable whenever possible.

Let's presume you now have a habit of making lists and you definitely don't play the list-losing game, but you find you just can't discipline yourself to make a list every day. That's OK. Many people find it difficult to write a list daily. Make up your mind to use lists when you're swamped, over- whelmed, or (God forbid) procrastinating.

≈

POP QUIZ

1. What are your most productive times of day?
2. Where are you most productive?
3. Does what or how much you eat affect your productivity? Do you feel sluggish after eating certain foods?
4. Does exercising affect your productivity? (Do you feel more energized on days you've "moved around"?)

≈

THOSE PRECIOUS POCKETS OF TIME

Obviously, everyone is allotted the same number of hours in a day. Why is it that some people never find time to do what they intend to do, and others can always find time to get things done?

One of the great secrets of high achievers and anticrastinators is that they are mindful that every day is jam-packed with an incredible number of precious pockets of time, if only you learn to recognize and use them. While the procrastinators lose valuable time waiting for a free hour to pay some bills, or a free afternoon to sort through stacks of papers and files, or a free Saturday to clean the garage or to connect with a fellow human or whatever (fill in the blank), the anticrastinators accept four universal truths:

1. Free hours, afternoons, or entire days hardly ever come into our lives without a great deal of scheming and planning; even then, don't count on it.
2. No matter how important your project is or how much preplanning went into it, there will be interruptions. Lots of them. Count on it.
3. Complaining about interruptions and letting them stress you out won't help anything and won't make the interruptions go away. Sometimes we can eliminate the source of our interruptions (take the phone off the hook, do our work at the library, close the office door). Sometimes we can't.
4. If interruptions continually cause you to start and stop your project, you may as well plan on working in starts and stops.

During phone calls, Juanita takes advantage of the time when she is put on hold. She reads from a book she keeps on her desk filled with short, creative sales and marketing tips.

Barb has to cross several train tracks near her house whenever she drives anywhere. She frequently finds herself sitting in her car waiting for a train to pass. During this downtime, she jots a few lines to friends or clients. (She keeps in her car a large Ziploc bag filled with note cards, a pen, and stamps.) They enjoy hearing from her and read their "snail mail" several times, as opposed to their E-mail messages, which they just glance over and delete.

Barb's husband, Charlie, uses his "train-waiting time" to record ideas in his voice-activated recorder, which he keeps under the car seat.

Even on your busiest days, you have a spare ten minutes here, twenty minutes there. How much time could you put to good use if you worked on your lists or began ten-minute projects while waiting for a meeting to begin or for a dental appointment, or while sitting in your car waiting for your child to come out of school? You could:

- plan
- review your list
- make a phone call (cell phones make this feasible almost anywhere)
- catch up on correspondence
- outline a news release, report, letter, or book
- skim a magazine and decide whether it's worth your time.

Right now—starting today—watch for a precious pocket of time and decide how you're going to use it. A glance at your list can help you figure out what to do with this time. Amazingly, the more you recognize and use these precious pockets of time, the more they seem to multiply.

THE LIVELY ART OF BACK TIMING

Another excellent strategy to use when you're feeling overwhelmed is to set interim deadlines. The objective is to work backward by setting fake or target deadlines for yourself. My husband, Bruce, a videotape editor, calls it "back timing."

Consider the following situations:

- The boss wants that newsletter completed and on his desk tomorrow, and you haven't even decided what to write about.
- Today is April 14, and you haven't started working on your income tax yet.
- Christmas is two days away, and you haven't even thought about what gifts to buy.
- Your final exam is tomorrow afternoon, and you still haven't reviewed your notes.
- Labor pains are five minutes apart, and you haven't packed for the hospital yet.

In each case, the impending deadline sends us spinning off in a flurry of activity. Deadlines stop our procrastination; they get our adrenaline pumping; they motivate us. Of course, they also strike fear in our hearts, tie our stomachs in knots, cause hyperventilation (and sometimes splotches on our skin, headaches, insomnia; or some other disaster), but they do get us moving.

The way to accentuate the positive of deadlines and eliminate the negative stress associated with them is to set many minideadlines. Though they may feel artificial at first, they'll help you become organized, they'll make the project manageable, and they'll force you to think things through ahead of time. This way of planning eventually becomes a habit.

Setting artificial or target deadlines also eliminates those situations where you're heading down the final stretch and you discover that you desperately need something, but it's too late to get it. For example: You have only one day to develop your sales presentation. All's well because you know you can get it done in a day. Then terror strikes when you realize Ivan is the only person who can give you some absolutely necessary statistics . . . and Ivan left for vacation yesterday. An artificial deadline would have saved the day.

How does this artificial deadline work? You start at the real deadline and work backward to the present, setting interim deadlines for accomplishing part or all of your project. You "back-time" it. Let's say you want to run a news release in the local weekly paper about your company's support of a fund-raiser taking place on May 30. You check the calendar and decide you want your article run one week earlier, in the May 23 issue. You call the paper and find out that your article must be at least a week ahead of time in order to be included in that particular issue. This means it must be in the mail by the eleventh or twelth. You set yourself a deadline to write it by May 5, which allows enough time to have it typed, proofread, and mailed by the eleventh. If you had not set interim deadlines, you probably wouldn't have even started thinking about writing it until it was too late.

By starting at the deadline and working backward, you come up with a chronological work list. Sometimes, when people are planning a wedding, someone will hand them a list, explaining, "Six months ahead of time, do this. Five months ahead of time, do that." Unfortunately, we aren't lucky enough to have people handing us itemized work lists for our everyday projects, but we can make them ourselves—by thinking backward, by back timing.

Once you get in the habit of back timing, you'll find it applies to numerous activities. "The plane takes off at five o'clock, we have to be at the airport at four, so we'll plan to leave by three o'clock. Let's see, we have your sister staying with us; that's an extra person jockeying to use the bathroom; so let's all start getting ready by half past one."

When approaching a project backward, use your imagination to visualize what's happening. It will help you think of details that could head off disaster. When planning to write your report, for example, imagine what you'll need to have when you get started. Then set a deadline ahead of time to gather all the vital materials you'll need, rather than starting on the report and then hitting the panic button.

Whether you think backward naturally or have to work at it, developing the habit of back timing will make a project more manageable, help you anticipate obstacles, and eliminate most of that last-minute, knot-in-the-stomach stress.

Whatever system you decide to use when you're feeling overwhelmed, don't cop out by sleeping, surfing the Web, reading, playing computer games, eating, watching TV, sorting through stuff, or whatever you do when you procrastinate. Instead, break down the job into little steps, prioritize, and then begin by taking that first single step.

Thoughts to Consider

At any given time we are actually the best we can be at that time.

—Wayne Dyer

Lakein's Question: What is the best use of my time right now?

—Alan Lakein

The person who wastes today lamenting yesterday will waste tomorrow lamenting today.

—Philip M. Raskin

Here is a test to find whether your mission on earth is finished—if you're alive, it isn't.

—Richard Bach

The really unhappy people are the ones who leave undone what they can do, and start doing what they don't understand; no wonder they come to grief.

—Johann Wolfgang von Goethe

I'd rather be a failure at something I love than a success at something I hate.

—George Burns

Success is never final, failure is never fatal; it is courage that counts.

—*Winston Churchill*

You don't set the course for where you are going until you know where you are.

—*Unknown*

Even if you're on the right track, you'll get run over if you just sit there.

—*Will Rogers*

EXTRA CREDIT

This exercise is an intriguing way to back-time, as well as to set up a life plan. You can do it many times, as your goals and priorities change.

Imagine yourself as you would like to be ten years from now. Then fill in the following as if today were that date:

• Date (ten years from today): _____

• Where you live: _____

_____

• What you're doing: _____

_____

• Whom you're with: _____

_____

• Where you have traveled: _____

_____

• Your proudest moment in the last ten years: _____

_____

• A typical Saturday: _____

_____

• Things you own: _____

_____

• How you've changed as a person: _____

_____

Now go back and name one thing you can do in the next
year to bring yourself closer to each of these goals in ten
years. What can you do by next week?

PART III

Proven Strategies for Conquering Procrastination

7

"Plan Time to Plan!"

❧

A VERY POPULAR STYLE of procrastination is called "plunging"; it is derived from the ancient phrase "Nuts with planning; I'll plunge right in."

Unfortunately, when you plunge into a job without doing any planning, you frequently sabotage the whole project because: (1) many things go wrong, and the job drags out much longer than is necessary; (2) you become so aggravated because nothing works out that you leave the job unfinished and forget about it; (3) once you've completed the project, you've established a negative mind-set, so that every time you think about doing this project again, you delay starting it because you have such dreadful memories of how long it took or how exasperating a chore it was to do.

Sean continually plunges into fixing his car without giving any thought to the repair ahead of time. As a result, he tears the car apart, then discovers he needs to buy something. Since it's usually difficult to drive a car that is torn apart, Sean has to figure out a way to go pick up the part he needs. He has to find someone who will either run the errand for him or drive him to the store. Of course, he runs into hassles. He has to wash some grease off his hands before he goes to the store, and more than once he has arrived at the auto parts store only to find it closed. Then he has to go back and either put the car together without fixing it or leave it until the next day and then spend the rest of the day without the use of his car. Needless to say, Sean hates working on the car and puts it off whenever he can.

A few minutes' worth of thought before plunging into an auto project could save Sean a great deal of time, energy, and frustration. With a little planning, he might be able to anticipate what he needs for a repair job, or at least check out ahead of time whether the auto parts store will be open and be sure someone is available to drive him there.

≈≈

QUICK TIP

Set aside planning
time each day.

≈≈

The Planning Process

To plan for a project, you don't need charts or graphs or committee meetings (although that type of planning can be helpful for some jobs). The planning I'm talking about is simply setting aside a little time to think about what tools or resources you'll need, and how you're going to tackle the project at hand.

A good way to remember these steps is:

> Time to think
> Write with ink
> Conversation
> Imagination.

We've just covered the first step, "time to think." Let's now look at each of the other steps in turn.

Write with Ink

What do I mean by "write with ink"? Make a list. Get it in writing. As long as your plan is floating around in your brain, it's muddy, and you don't see details. Mark Victor Hansen, coauthor of *Chicken Soup for the Soul*, says, "Don't think it, ink it."

Once you write out your "planning list," you'll find that it tends to be one of two types: either a list of things to do, which you can prioritize, or a "need list" consisting of tools and purchases necessary to move the project along. For example, you might write "do grocery shopping" on your to-do list and prepare a separate list of the various foods you need to buy.

Sue produces special events for more than 1,000 employees at the corporate office of a Milwaukee brewery, and she uses a two-list system for every event. For example, when planning the holiday party, she might use the following to-do list: select theme, set committee meetings, obtain entertainment, meet with caterer, order gifts for children, get decorations, design marketing pieces, and obtain photographer. She also posts above her desk a list of over fifteen items to be ordered or purchased, including toys for the various age groups of children, floral centerpieces, party favors, candy canes, balloons, and thank-you gifts for people who help plan the party. This way, when she's ready to place the orders, everything is written in one place. If it was all on her to-do list, she'd have to keep copying all those items over and over until the time was right to make the purchase. Besides, she found that adding the fifteen or twenty items to be purchased to her to-do list made it overwhelming.

Conversation

Conversation entails talking about your project or task with others and then listening. You might be surprised at the helpful tips and techniques, ideas and encouragement you receive. Someone might offer to lend you equipment that will make the job easier. Who knows? Someone might even offer to help you work on your project.

For years, Taylor had wanted to switch careers but never knew how, or what to do about it. Finally, she decided, as preparation for a "career-change plan," to start talking to her friends about the subject. She was amazed at the solid advice she received, and delighted when a friend told her of a job opening and then helped her set up an interview. She landed the job and says that if she had known that her career change would occur this smoothly, she certainly wouldn't have procrastinated all those years. Another advantage of conversation: Sometimes when you're stumped or confused about something, simply talking about the problem generates the solution.

Imagination

One of the greatest planning tools is your imagination. Take a few minutes to mentally picture doing the job; imagine each step of the project, each tool or paper or form needed, each person involved, and what you might need from that person. Once you visualize doing what you need to do, you'll be amazed at how smoothly the work flows along.

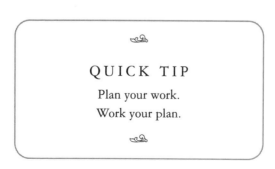

QUICK TIP

Plan your work.
Work your plan.

Recently John, a minister, called and asked me to present a seminar at his church. The date he requested was right in the middle of an extremely busy week, and I wasn't sure if I could add this seminar to my schedule. "Let me picture living through that week, and I'll get back to you," I told him. After studying my calendar and giving that week some imagination time, I called him and agreed to the date.

He told me that he loved my concept of imagining living through a busy time period in my schedule. After our initial phone conversation, he had received four requests to attend different functions. Each time John told the other person that he wanted to imagine what his day or week would be like if he accommodated his or her request. He then took a few minutes to visualize that time period and was able to make a more realistic decision about his schedule. He avoided the frenzy that results from saying yes to anything that sounds like fun (or something we "should" do) but that overburdens us when the time comes to actually do it.

Silvia's story illustrates the problems that can arise from not using your imagination when there's a job to be done. She worked as a receptionist for a group of pediatricians, who asked her if she would be willing to decorate the waiting room. Sylvia gladly agreed because she loved doing that type of thing. The doctors wanted their young patients to enjoy the festive sense of celebrating for weeks before each upcoming holiday. They supplied wonderful sparkling hearts for St. Valentine's Day, charming shamrocks for St. Patrick's Day, and chubby turkeys for Thanksgiving. Sylvia loved their selections, yet she would procrastinate and the decorations often went up only three or four days before the holiday.

Sylvia would apologize and tell the doctors that this time she'd been swamped and next time the decorations would go up much earlier. The frustrated doctors asked her if she thought this should not be part of her job. "Not at all," protested Sylvia.

"Would you like to go out and select different decorations?" they asked her.

Again Sylvia protested, "No, I love what we have." But she honestly didn't know *why* she would wait till the last minute to decorate.

In fact, the job was a real pain in the neck for Sylvia, and she was avoiding it because she dreaded it. She'd climb the stepladder, then climb down to get masking tape. Then climb the stepladder again. Then down again for a pair of scissors. Sometimes she had to search the premises to find a glue stick or the right color marker. She'd be up and down that ladder twelve times putting up simple decorations. The job took much longer than necessary, and Sylvia would work up a sweat doing it. The next day her legs and feet would ache.

Sylvia could have turned things around with just a little bit of planning. She could have pictured in her imagination everything necessary for the task, gathered up what she needed, bought what was missing (extra tape measure, thumbtacks, a hammer, nails, all kinds of tapes), and put everything in a small fishing tackle box that she could have carried everywhere, including up the ladder. This would have immediately ended all the running around and climbing up and down; it would have cut the decorating time in half; and, most important of all, it would have eliminated the source of Sylvia's frustration.

By using her imagination in the planning process, Sylvia might have found herself once again enjoying the process of decorating.

୧୨

QUICK TIP

If you fail to plan,
You plan to fail.

୧୨

A COUPLE OF EXPERT PLANNERS

Lucy and Jack are both expert planners. When they remodeled their house last year, they spent a great deal of time and thought planning their work. They wrote a to-do list covering every aspect of the job that they could think of, a "need list" of tools and purchases, and then they set up a Portable Project Center with a spiral notebook in a pocket folder. (See chapter 6.)

Almost once a week, they'd sit together and make up a weekly (sometimes daily) to-do list, jotting down each step of the next tasks to be accomplished. They'd decide who would do what and when, and then check if they needed to buy any tools, equipment, or materials.

Lucy and Jack also made good use of the planning steps of conversation and imagination. Besides talking to each other, they would give anyone who asked a summary of upcoming projects. A friend at work offered Jack the use of his electric staple gun for installing insulation, and Jack's sister offered to watch their children while they put up wallpaper.

Lucy's practice of vividly visualizing each step of her tasks enabled her to prioritize and head off potential trouble. For example, at one point before the wallboard went up, Lucy was picturing furniture in one room and realized that a corner of that room would need more light. Before it was too late, she and Jack were able to install a small octagonal window in that corner. By combining imagination and planning, not only did Lucy and Jack finish their remodeling project efficiently, they were enormously pleased with the outcome.

Life becomes so much easier when you develop the habit of planning, instead of plunging into tasks unprepared. Work goes smoother and is completed quicker, plus the quality of the finished project usually improves. Next time you're facing a project, take a few minutes to think it through, put your lists and ideas in writing, talk about your project to others, and use that most wonderful, most remarkable planning tool, your imagination.

Once you become a planner—as opposed to a "plunger"—you will start gaining control of your procrastination problem.

෴

Thoughts to Consider

Every moment spent planning saves three or four in execution.

—Crawford Greenwalt

By recording your dreams and goals on paper, you set in motion the process of becoming the person you most want to be.

—Mark Victor Hansen

If you do not know where you are going, every road will get you nowhere.

—Henry Kissinger

If you must begin then go all the way, because if you begin and quit, the unfinished business you have left behind begins to haunt you all the time.

—Chogyam Trungpa

The indispensable first step to getting the things you want out of life is this: Decide what you want.

—Ben Stein

You must have long-range goals to keep you
from being frustrated by short-range failures.

—Charles C. Noble

Everything you want is out there waiting for you
to ask. Everything you want also wants you. But
you have to take action to get it.

—Jack Canfield

If you aim at nothing, you're sure to hit it.

—Unknown

EXTRA CREDIT

1. What do you hope to have achieved with your life five
   years from now? _____

   _____

2. What plans, priorities, and hopes would you like to realize by a year from now? _____

   _____

3. What is your plan for the next month? _____

   _____

4. What is your plan for this coming week? _____

_____

5. What is your plan for today? _____

_____

8

Clutter Busting

_ﾟゃ_

TIME MANAGEMENT HAS changed over the years. Recently a speaker said, "The old time management was the advice to 'handle each piece of paper only once.' It's time to toss out the old advice and bring in the new." Well, I wouldn't be so quick to toss out any of the old time management principles.

A desk overflowing with papers can bring all productivity to a screeching halt and throw procrastination into high gear. Clutter creates a vicious circle. On the one hand, you put off sorting through papers and getting rid of clutter; but on the other hand, this same clutter and chaos often contribute to and increase your procrastination.

Shirley, a seminar participant who worked for a government agency, described how she and her staff were each doing the work of two or more people, with reduced resources and a diminished support staff. Papers on her desk used to pile up in huge stacks. She said that when she first read the line about handling each piece of paper only once in Alan Lakein's *How to Get Control of Your Time and Your Life,* she realized that she spent far too much time shuffling through the same papers over and over. So Shirley wrote Lakein's advice, "Handle each piece of paper only once," on an index card and stuck it on the wall above her stacks of papers to remind her to stop shuffling and to decide what to do with each piece of paper the first time she handled it. Now it's become a habit. Every once in a while, she catches herself doing the paper shuffle again, and she uses Lakein's advice to get herself back on track.

The "old" time management principles are still valid, and there's no reason to abandon them. But times change, and we have some new and different time management needs these days. The story of our time today is that there will always be too much to do, too much to read, too much new information to try to absorb. Our new time challenges call for some new rules to help us manage our time:

- You can't do it all.
- You can't read it all.
- You can't learn it all.

YOU CAN'T READ EVERYTHING

Lots of rules resounding in your head from earlier times no longer apply. For example, in second grade your teacher may have told you, "Don't skip words. Read every single word on that page in front of you. Every single word!"

Well, it's time to throw out that rule from grade school. Our grandparents—maybe even our parents—were able to read every piece of mail, every memo, newsletter, newspaper, magazine, and mail-order catalog that interested them. You can't. No one can these days. Until you accept that fact, you'll be creating a lose/lose situation. Either you'll feel like a loser for procrastinating about all your unread papers, or in the time spent trying to read everything, you'll feel like a loser because you've put off some of the really important things in your life.

Shirley, as she continued talking about the overwhelming amount of paper in her office, said that every once in a while, she surveys the stacks of paper coming into her life and sighs, "Pages and pages of information everywhere—but not one word of wisdom."

It's time to accept the fact that the only way to read everything you want is to drop out of life, become a hermit, and spend every waking moment speed-reading. The watchword for today is *prioritize.* Select what is important to read and don't sweat the rest.

PAPER, PAPER, EVERYWHERE

Look around at all the paper in your life. Do you have stacks of papers, memos, professional journals, newsletters, magazines, catalogs, and junk mail growing at work or in your house? Do you fear that future generations of children may not know what trees look like because they are all being cut down and turned into paper (the trees, not the children) and being stuffed into your mailbox or splattered across your desk? Do you stare at your paper clutter, feeling hopeless and helpless about where to begin? Do you start off tackling your paper clutter with determination and eventually wind up whimpering in a corner curled up in a fetal position? The more that people predict we will soon have a "paperless office," the more paper clutter we seem to accumulate in our lives.

Earlier we covered "taking small single steps" when we are overwhelmed, but this principle doesn't always work when it comes to sorting through papers. You can't just sit and sort, and be done with it. If you don't go ahead and file, toss, recycle, process, or put each paper where it belongs, you won't accomplish anything. You'll only end up having to sort through the whole pile again. The secret is to move your body. You have to stand up and walk around delivering your papers to their proper spots. Let this become your motto, and follow it frequently:

Sit and sort
Stand and deliver

If you don't have a place to put your papers and files, create a place to put everything *ahead* of time. Even if you have to put your files in a cardboard box and shove it in a closet or under your desk or bed, at least when you're finished sorting, you'll have a place to put and store your stacks of paper.

Your Friend
the Wastebasket

To conquer paper clutter, you need to change your attitude about your wastebasket. It is not an enemy who gobbles up all your important data. It is your friend who needs to be nurtured and fed. So feed your wastebasket.

In fact, buy or make several wastebaskets—one for every area where paper accumulates. They come in attractive colors and styles, but don't buy little bitty dainty ones unless you have little bitty dainty stacks of papers. Mega–paper clutter requires mega-wastebaskets. Lots of them.

As you start streamlining your paper accumulation, you can apply the same principles to computer clutter. You'll begin to find it easier to put old, unnecessary E-mail, files, directories, jokes, cartoons, and poems in the trash can.

Once you accept that your world won't end when you courageously throw out paper clutter, you will no longer be overwhelmed, immobilized, and catapulted into procrastination by all that reading material coming into your life. And you will have something new to look forward to: the joy of feeding your wastebasket.

"Too-Much-of-a-Good-Thing" Magazines

Now for one of my favorite clutter questions, one that people should ask themselves at least once a year: Would you pay money, would you pay your hard-earned cash, to increase your paper clutter? Most of you would say, "No, never! I hate this paper clutter. Why would I pay to add to it?"

Well, that's exactly what you are doing each time you subscribe to a magazine you don't really want or need. How do you decide if you've subscribed to a "too-much-of-a-good-thing" magazine? When your magazine arrives in the mail, do you shout, "Hooray! It's here! I'm going to read it before I fall asleep tonight"? Or do you mumble, "Oh, good . . . another issue. I'll read it after I catch up on the past six months' worth that I haven't found time to read"?

Ask yourself, "Why did I buy this magazine?" Did you buy it for the technical articles? The health tips? The recipes? Investment information? If so, then tear out the articles you need, file them away, and toss the magazine into your friendly wastebasket or recycling bin. Did you buy it to read every single word? If so, do you have time to read the entire issue each month? If you do, there's no problem. If you don't have the time, stop and reevaluate the situation. Would you be better off buying a copy at a store or newsstand every few months when you do have the time to enjoy it, rather than letting back issues accumulate and feeling guilty? Did you buy the magazine because it contains important information that is necessary for your career or hobby? Then set up a place to store or file the issues and accept the fact that you don't have time to read every word, but they are available as reference material.

Herman used to store several boxes of electronics magazines in his workshop. After attending my Conquer Procrastination seminar, he realized he didn't want to be caretaker of those boxes anymore, and he could use the space for other things. He discovered that the library kept on file all the back issues of the magazines he subscribed to, so he happily tossed out all his old copies. Now when Herman needs information on electronics, the reference librarian helps him track it down in much less time than it would take him to search through each of his old magazines. And if he does feel like thumbing through a few back issues, he can do it at the library and not add to his paper clutter. (Ironically, this electronics guru doesn't have a computer. Wait till he discovers all the information available to him on the Internet.)

Another seminar participant, Sandy, helped some friends move to a new house. Among all the boxes were eighteen years' worth of *National Geographic* magazines. The couple had been married only ten years, but his father had passed along eight years' worth of magazines to them. (What a guy!) She asked them if they thought the *National Geographic* collections would become valuable someday. They said, "No, but the pictures are so wonderful, we just can't throw them out." Sandy admitted that the pictures were wonderful, but eighteen years' worth led to a lot of boxes. Heavy boxes!

If you have the space to store magazines and you are happy to be the caretaker of them, that's fine. You have no problem. But if you are ready to let go of them, consider donating them to a hospital or a library or to your doctor's office. Perhaps a teacher or Scout leader could use magazines with wonderful photos. Or simply put them in a recycling bin. I'm not suggesting that you throw out important or sentimental or meaningful issues of magazines. Just the ones that are cluttering up your life—issues that you know you'll never read or need.

THIS IS YOUR LAST CATALOG

We can't omit the topic of catalogs. You know the ones I mean. When the first few arrived, you were fascinated by all the adorable gadgets. Then your name magically was sold to every catalog company in the world, and now you need a bigger mailbox to hold them. My neighbor Ellen once showed me a week's worth of catalogs delivered to her house. To her amazement, she and her husband had received catalogs for garden stuff, kitchen stuff, travel stuff, whale stuff (yes, whales), kid stuff, Irish stuff, international stuff, writer's stuff, music box stuff, and general stuff. Ellen said she used to be afraid that if she didn't look through each catalog, she'd miss some sensational item.

Trust me: If you miss it, you'll have another chance to buy it when the next catalog comes and the next. Ellen received one with the notice: "This is your last chance. If you don't order now, your name may be removed from our mailing list." That one company sent her seven last chances.

If you simply cannot throw out catalogs without looking through them, but you don't have the time to read them so you keep adding them to your piles of paper clutter, here's what you do: Set them aside without looking through any of them until you've collected a big stack. Then go through a week's or a month's worth all at once. The first few, you'll look at every page. Then you'll start to skip pages. Eventually, you'll decide to toss some out without even looking at them.

Behold the Pack Rat

In addition to being paper clutterers, a high percentage of procrastinators are pack rats who collect and save a wide assortment of ordinary or wonderfully weird things.

When procrastinators attending a Conquer Procrastination seminar hear the question "Why do people put off throwing out their clutter?" they just sit there, smiling, blinking, having absolutely no idea what the question means. The reason they are bewildered is they *don't* consider their clutter to be a procrastination issue. They aren't putting off tossing out their things; they never even think about getting rid of them, even if all these assorted possessions are needlessly complicating their lives.

The question has to be: "Why do people hang on to their clutter?" And the answers usually fit into one of these categories:

1. I love my clutter.
2. I might need it someday.
3. I can never throw away anything.

Seminar participants admit that it would be better if they had less clutter in their lives. (In some cases, being a pack rat has serious consequences, especially when the clutter is driving the pack rat's partner crazy.) They are almost always eager to discuss each of their reasons for hanging on to their treasures. During the discussion, they gradually come to the conclusion that they would rather get rid of their clutter. But that decision only comes *after* they've explored their reasons for hanging on to their cherished stuff.

Reason 1: I Love My Clutter

Sometimes the truth is we have memories of loving our clutter. Many of our treasures gave us real joy or fulfilled a need a long time ago, but our needs have changed and these treasures are no longer a source of joy, especially when we have to keep dusting and cleaning them or finding places to store them. So ask yourself if you still want to be caretaker of all this stuff.

When I first started doing battle with my clutter, I discovered I had a severe disability: sentimentality. Sentimentality is the curse of clutterers. If I were having a good time someplace, I'd be determined to buy a souvenir, save a program or ticket stub, or acquire other mementos to remind me of this good time. I'm not talking beautiful paintings hanging on the wall; no, I would save a little plastic penguin for which my son paid a quarter one beautiful spring day at the zoo many, many moons ago.

Our house was decorated with all kinds of wonderful things made by my kids, including ceramic turtles made in fourth-grade art class and wall plaques painted at Scout meetings. In addition, I had accumulated a large assortment of dust-catching knickknacks and books. (If there is such a thing as a "bookaholic," I was one. I seldom walked past a bookstore without stopping and going inside. To me, bookstores are like giant vacuum cleaners; they just suck me right in. And, of course, I wouldn't think of leaving a bookstore without buying something.) I'm still not clear why I bought all those books. What I do know is that I never got around to reading many of them.

The ones I did finish reading either were passed on to friends or were "keepers," which found a special spot in a bookcase. But sometimes I'd read only part of a book, then stop. Instead of treating it as a "finished book," I would put it on a special "guilt shelf" of books I intended to finish reading someday. Then there were the books I never read, never referred to, never needed, never wanted. When I started clutter busting my house, I discovered there were more books in that last category than I care to admit.

As I rummaged through all my books and other accumulations, I asked myself the following questions:

- Maybe I loved this once, but do I still love it?
- Maybe I needed this once, but do I still need it?
- Maybe this brought joy to me once, but does it still bring joy as I dust it and look for places to put it and feel overwhelmed by having this and so many other things taking up space in my home? Do I really want to be a caretaker of this?

Finally, I gritted my teeth and started making decisions. If something was still wonderful, it stayed. If it was no longer wonderful, it went. Semiwonderful things also went, because I had an overabundance of wonderful things.

Twelve Tips for Having Less Chaos at Home

1. Have company over once in a while so the house gets cleaned.
2. Use your TV time to pay bills, fold laundry, sort through catalogs and magazines, and so forth.
3. Tidy up during commercials.
4. When decluttering a room, start at the doorway and go right or left. Then, if you're interrupted, you can pick up where you left off.
5. Don't declutter and clean on the same day. You might keel over, poor thing.
6. Keep all your house information (insurance, warranties, receipts, directions to program VCR) together in a file, binder, drawer, desk, box, or paper bag.
7. Never climb stairs empty-handed as long as there's something that should be taken upstairs.
8. Never leave a room empty-handed until the only items in the room are ones that belong there.
9. Glance over your left shoulder every time you leave a room. Pick up the clutter you spot and take it with you.
10. Learn to delegate.
11. Learn to ignore. Relationships are more important than chasing dust bunnies.
12. Hire someone to clean your house even if it's only once in a great while.

Today, some—but certainly not all—of my books are gone. Many of the souvenirs are gone. Most of the dust-catching knickknacks are gone. But my house is still decorated with fourth-grade ceramics, Scout wall plaques, and neat homemade things. I'm happy.

Oh, yes, the little plastic penguin is still with us. And probably always will be.

Reason 2: I Might Need It Someday

Many pack rats apply this reason to any item with the word *old* in front of it. "Someday, I might really need . . . old appliances, buttons, textbooks, clothes, broken toys, pieces of wood, wallboard or paneling, cookware, rusty nails, curtains, empty tape dispensers, film containers, car parts, and these three plates and one cup from my old set of dishes." But when was the last time someone called you asking to borrow some old, faded curtains? If you haven't needed any of these things yet and you don't need them now, why would you ever need them in the future?

If you work with cars and you actually do use old auto parts, or if you actually do have a use for old buttons, that's different. Or if you're saving something because it has value or is a collectible, again, that's different. But first find out more about its value or potential value. You might discover that you are putting hundreds of dollars' worth of time and effort into taking care of items that fifty years from now will bring you $17.43 if you are lucky.

If you've never needed one of those old things you've been accumulating, how can you rationalize keeping all of them? Even if you did need one of those old things, would you remember you had it or would you be able to find it among all the clutter?

Consider the following scenario: Your toaster breaks. You buy yourself a new toaster. What do you do with the old one? Throw it out? No. You store it away someplace— "Because I might need it if the new one breaks." But the old one is broken!

The procrastinator's reply: "Well, I might be able to use a part from the old one to fix the new one." Years ago, that was a valid premise. People would cannibalize an old appliance to obtain parts to fix the new one. If your TV broke, your neighbor could rummage around in the dusty corners of his garage, find a tube in an old TV set, put it in yours, and your TV would work. But those days are over. With today's high-tech appliances, parts simply are no longer interchangeable.

How about some of the other things you "might need later"? When your clothes become faded or ripped, do you save them to wear while painting the house or bathing the dog? We all need an outfit or two for doing grubby chores, but nobody needs a whole wardrobe of such clothes.

And how about all those too-small clothes you are saving to wear "when I lose some weight"? Will you really wear them? Will they still be in style? If you do work at losing the weight, and become slender and svelte, wouldn't you feel you deserve some wonderful new clothes?

Here's another example: Have you saved your notes and textbooks from college or high school or past seminars you've attended because your kids or someone "might be able to use them someday"? Can you really picture your teenager going through a stack of your dusty, yellowed, illegible notes, and schoolbooks with photos of people with nerdy hairstyles, and saying, "Wow, thanks, I can really use these."

You may be reluctant to part with your stuff because you believe that "no matter what I throw out, the very next day I just know I'll need it." Well, what if you do someday need something you threw out? Or you wish you still had whatever it was? Chances are you could replace it if necessary. When you're considering whether to discard something, ask yourself how difficult it would be to find another. How much would it cost to buy? Then weigh the cost of replacing it (on the *remote chance* you might need to someday) against the time and energy and bother involved with being a caretaker for this item . . . which you may never need.

Yes, we all know that sinking feeling when you've hung on to your copy of the *Ten Commandments for Cats* for three years, then the day after you pitch it or delete it, a friend calls you and asks for a copy of it. You can calm that apprehension by telling yourself, "I'd love to take care of everybody's needs, but I can't be responsible for holding on to every item that comes my way just because someone, somewhere, someday might need it."

Once you experience the freedom of throwing out clutter and realizing that the world will not end the next day, it will become easier to face discarding items without worrying about needing those things in the future.

Reason 3: I Can Never Throw Anything Away

This seems to be one of the most basic reasons for pack rats to accumulate clutter. They don't cherish their junk or think they'll need it someday. They simply cannot throw it away.

If the idea of parting with any of your belongings causes you stress, don't give up. The first thing you should do is explore a few of the reasons some people can't throw anything away.

"You don't know what it was like growing up during the depression," I've been told by procrastinators who can't let go of their clutter. (Oddly, I also have heard this from people born twenty years after the depression.) Or, "When I was a kid, our family was very poor."

If hard times come into your life again, do you honestly think you're going to provide for your family with 178 old film containers or twelve broken toasters? Seriously, if you want to get rid of your clutter, but in spite of everything you've tried you simply cannot move it out, consider professional counseling.

Does your clutter give you a sense of financial security? Hanging on to clutter that you hate simply because it "might" be valuable someday doesn't make sense.

Instead take a more constructive approach to financial security. Start a habit today of putting a little money in a savings account each week. Just as small amounts of your stuff add up to a house full of clutter, so, too, do small amounts of money saved each week quickly add up to a nice-sized "nest egg," but with the opposite result. You will be so pleased with your improved finances and the feelings of security that go with it that you might be able to let go of some of the clutter that served as your "security blanket."

SAYING GOOD-BYE TO CLUTTER

If you're ready to start tackling your clutter, here are some ideas to ease you into "discard" mode. First, recognize the difference between what you should throw out and what you should keep. If you truly feel warm and secure and comfortable with your belongings, they're probably not clutter; they're a collection or a gathering of treasures. Keep them. Find a neat way to store or display them.

But be honest about how you feel. What once gave you comfort may no longer be a source of security. It may now be a pain in the neck. Here are three examples of people who reassessed their attitudes toward their possessions.

Jessica's collection of dolls and stuffed animals has increased over the years to the point of looking like clutter. On reflection, she decided each doll had a special story, a

Decluttering Tips

Get rid of the item if:

- you've always hated it
- you can't find it or forget you have it when you do need it
- it's broken or obsolete (and fixing it is unrealistic)
- it no longer satisfies a need
- it's the wrong size, wrong color, or wrong style
- you have to clean it, store it, insure it, or give it space, but you don't get much use or enjoyment from it
- using it is more bother than it's worth
- it wouldn't really affect you if you never saw it again.

Maybe keep the item if:

- you feel terrific keeping it
- it helps you make a living
- it has significant emotional or spiritual value to you
- you consider it to be useful
- it has significant cash value (you don't want to keep a ninety-five-cent comic book for fifty-seven years and get only $1.35 for it)
- it would be treasured by the next generation.

special memory that was still precious to her; therefore, she found a beautiful way to display the dolls behind glass, so they no longer collected dust. Then she tried cleaning up the stuffed animals, but it didn't work. So she decided to get rid of all except three because most of the stuffed animals had become faded and dirty looking, and no longer were a source of joy or comfort.

Tanner had a collection of sports trophies all over his house. At one time, they had meant a great deal to him; just looking at them brought him many happy memories. Now, years later, they have become less important to him. Rather than get rid of them, he has packed them away neatly in labeled boxes and has eliminated having to dust, clean, and take care of them, and worrying about the dogs knocking them over.

Shannon's garage contained practically every old broken appliance she had ever owned. She can no longer remember why she was keeping them all these years, but now she's decided she no longer wants to be the caretaker of all that clutter and it is time to get rid it.

HOW ARE YOU GOING TO GET RID OF YOUR CLUTTER?

Often, as seminar participants look at and discuss these various concepts, they start to recognize that a cluttered environment contributes to cluttered thinking, and cluttered thinking contributes to procrastination. So they decide (finally!) to start to get rid of their clutter. The question is: how?

There are dozens of ways to move clutter out of your life without actually walking to a garbage can and throwing your treasures into it. If you're a pack rat, putting items in the trash is not always the solution, because you might tiptoe out to the garbage cans at 2:00 A.M. and retrieve everything you've thrown out.

One way to dispose of excess stuff is to hold a garage sale, where people will actually pay you money for your clutter. But some individuals can't deal with the logistics and bother of setting up a sale, pricing items, and sitting in the garage for a whole weekend. Others can't handle the idea of people buying and walking away with their cherished possessions. It is truly a pathetic sight to watch a man running after a car trying to buy back his beloved moosehead.

If you can't deal with garage sales, for whatever reason, ask friends who are having one to let you include your items with theirs. In return, you could volunteer to help tag items or relieve the cashier for a few hours, or offer them a percentage of your profits.

One really satisfactory way to move clutter out of your home is to find a worthwhile charity that could use it. You could donate items for a church rummage sale or to an organization that will stop at your place several times a year to pick up your things, or that has a drop-off box at a location near you. Some groups will repair broken appliances or furniture; others won't. Some want only clothes, whereas others will take old eyeglasses, books, pet supplies, canceled stamps, or labels from soup cans. Ask around, or look through your yellow pages and call to see what items a particular agency will accept. Contact your city hall, church, library, or local family service agency to locate an organization that would find your clutter useful. In recycling your stuff, not only do you help others and yourself, you do a kindness for Mother Earth.

If you have decided to donate some items but you're still too attached to them to let them go, pack your things into bags or boxes, label them with today's date, and store them in a closet, basement, attic, garage, or corner of your bedroom. Then, six months from now (or whatever schedule you decide), take the boxes to an organization that will be delighted to receive your possessions. Don't look inside. If you haven't needed these things in the past months, you don't need them. If it's still too hard for you to part with the items, ask a friend to take the boxes away.

CALL A NON–PACK RAT FRIEND

If you are serious about clutter busting but you're having trouble getting started, you are probably overlooking one of the most wonderful resources available to you: friends. You might be amazed to know that not everyone saves and accumulates clutter. If you talk to a few friends, you will probably discover you know several people who are terrific at tossing out clutter, and who would be happy to help you with yours. How can they help you?

GIFTS, GIFTS,
AND MORE GIFTS

❧

You're more than willing to throw out that alligator skull lamp or the three-foot-high fertility ritual vase or the black velour sequined pillow sham from Las Vegas, but you can't because it was a gift from your parents. They'd notice if it weren't on display when they came to visit.

Well, sometimes you're just stuck with gifts, and there isn't much you can do about it. If you are extremely close to the gift giver, you might explain that you can't use the gift . . . but that takes masterful tact, and even then, you risk hurting someone you love. If a few years have passed since you received the gift, you might simply explain that it's time to move it out, pass it on, or replace it.

Since discarding an ugly or unwanted gift can be awkward, it's much better to take some preventive measures and try heading these gift givers off at the pass. When people ask you what you want for your birthday, do you answer, "Nothing"? Only two outcomes will result from this reply. Either they'll give you what you asked for (nothing), and that's fine—unless you didn't mean what you said. (Admit it. You're a *little* hurt when they do that, aren't you?) Or they'll give you something anyway, hoping it's something you'll like. Maybe you will; if so, lucky you. If not, you now have another item to add to the things that are already cluttering your home. You might as well face the fact that people *want* to give gifts, and they appreciate knowing what you want.

Patricia Connelley, a licensed marriage and family therapist in private practice, came up with a brilliant idea for her sixtieth birthday bash. She had invited a big crowd to her party, and she knew they couldn't imagine arriving without *something* to give her. Patricia honestly did not want any gifts; she already had all her house could hold. So on her invitations, she asked her friends to bring food for the local food pantry. The day after the party, she delivered several hundred pounds of food to an agency that helps people in need. This turned out to be a win/win idea for everyone: Patricia, her friends (who could not have arrived empty-handed), and, most of all, many needy people.

When your gift givers ask you what you'd like for an occasion, *tell them*. If they don't ask, let them know that you'd be glad to offer some ideas or suggestions. Be specific. Give them a description of the item you want and tell them what store you've seen it in. Or pick several items in a range of prices from a catalog, so givers will have a choice, and you will receive something you'll really like.

If you feel you don't need or want any more things around your home, ask for:

- a membership to a museum, zoo, or some cultural group
- a gift certificate for a dinner or a brunch or a massage or an ice cream sundae
- tickets to a show or play
- a book you can read and then give to a friend or the library
- a contribution to a favorite charity.

Don't let yourself become miserable because well-meaning people who love you keep giving you things you neither need nor want. To become a good clutter buster and a gracious recipient, you have to communicate creatively and gently with the people who care enough to offer their gifts.

They can offer encouragement to help you truly believe that you can let go of your junk without disastrous consequences. Also, they can help you decide what you can live without. Hope, who attended my seminar, said one of her first attempts at clutter busting was an attack on her closet. She asked a friend, Sandra, to sit with a cup of coffee and encourage her to get rid of at least half the clothes she never wore. Sandra would ask, "How long since you've worn that?" If Hope answered, "I never wear it," Sandra advised, "Get rid of it."

Hope needed her friend for only one sitting. After that, she could look at hardly worn clothes and admit all by herself that buying them had been a mistake. Now she thinks more carefully before she makes a purchase. And when she does make a mistake, she tries to return the item right away rather than letting it hang in her closet for years.

Once you discover a friend who loves to declutter, loves to streamline, loves to organize, and who is willing to help guide you, you may not even need her or him to come over to your place. Simply reporting your progress by phone will be an enormous incentive to you.

Each step you take in conquering procrastination leads you to a greater sense of freedom, and taking control of your papers and your clutter can often make you stronger in managing your time and your life. You also may notice your step feels just a bit lighter as you walk your journey.

Tips for Paper Clutter

- Feed the wastebasket.
- Get rid of what you don't need.
- Skim material as soon as it arrives.
- Don't even skim junk mail; just toss it.
- Pass on to the appropriate person any papers someone else can handle.
- Find a place for everything worth keeping, and put the papers where they belong.
- Realize the world won't end if you get rid of something.
- Recycle paper.
- Ask yourself: Do you really want to be caretaker of this paper? Do you really want to devote precious space to clutter?

㊢

㊢

Thoughts to Consider

Life is not a having and a getting, but a being and a doing.

—Unknown

There must be more to life than having everything.

—Maurice Sendak

Not what we have, but what we enjoy, constitutes our abundance.

—John Petit-Senn

The best things in life usually are not things.

—Anonymous

Until you make peace with who you are, you'll never be content with what you have.

—Doris Mortman

If we can't do great things we can do small things in a great way.

—Unknown

While we are postponing, life speeds by.

—Seneca

Motivation is when your dreams put on work clothes.

—Hal Roach

You must do the thing you think you cannot do.

—Eleanor Roosevelt

If I haven't used it in a year, it can't be too vital to my lifestyle.

—Rita Emmett

EXTRA CREDIT

Take a look at your clutter (not someone else's) in the following places:

- yard
- car
- living/family room
- kitchen, including recipe box
- dining room table
- bathroom, including medicine cabinet
- bedroom
- garage
- basement/attic
- spare room
- drawers and cabinets
- closets
- desk
- bookcases
- storage locker
- purse/wallet
- briefcase

Is this stuff really important? Do you need it? Can you live without it? Do you want to take care of it? Give it space? Look at it? Live with it? Clean it? Decide now.

EXTRA, EXTRA CREDIT

Spend fifteen minutes each day for the next week separating your paper clutter; then toss, file, reply, act on/decide, or recycle it.

Do it!

9

Dollars and Sense

⌘

IT MAY SURPRISE YOU to know that procrastination can have a tremendous impact on your wallet. However, the mere mention of money causes many people to immediately shift into procrastinating mode. Do you put off even thinking about finances? Do you delay paying bills or balancing your checkbook? Have you been meaning to start a savings or investment plan? Does the income tax deadline always cause a flurry of last-minute running around, as you try to find receipts and tax forms, then rush to the post office at the eleventh hour?

Every April 15, local stations in Chicago televise the scene of cars jammed up for blocks around the main post office as people drop off their tax returns in time to be postmarked before the deadline. The drivers usually appear more stressed out than relieved. Most, when interviewed, say that next year they will definitely start their taxes earlier.

Several years ago Eddie, who was building a successful business in network marketing, called me for advice because he always procrastinated about doing his taxes. He sighed and said, "I know how to build a business, how to market, how to manage people, and how to sell the products. But I dread tax time so much that I put everything off till the last minute and do a terrible job." He was exhausted and frustrated from tearing his house apart looking for all the paperwork he needed for his income tax records. He went on to describe his first meeting with his accountant. Eddie brought all the receipts in a grocery bag. The accountant looked at it and laughed.

A CURE FOR THOSE INCOME TAX BLUES

Like most people who dread doing income tax returns, Eddie needed to start with the old adage "A place for everything and everything in its place." He already had files to keep his bills and receipts in, so if he needed to refer to them throughout the year, he could find them. His problems began with the miscellaneous papers that would start accumulating in mid-January: tax forms, slips of interest paid and interest earned, statements of income received and money paid out, articles and memos with tax tips, and other tax-related paperwork that didn't have a file assigned to it. These papers wound up scattered throughout the house.

Part of Eddie's problem was he didn't have space for an office and his business was growing by leaps and bounds.

He optimistically told me that since two of his children were teenagers, they would no doubt be leaving the nest soon and he would have a spare room to use as an office. I didn't have the heart to tell him that many young people today are not eager to leave home, and some "go forth and multiply" and then return home.

Eddie decided to tackle his procrastination problem for several reasons:

- He was tired of the jokes and ribbing from his brothers and friends about his last-minute tax returns.
- He wanted his business associates to take him seriously. He didn't feel or look very professional when he was a maniac racing to meet that deadline.
- He was more prone to making mistakes and forgetting important details when he waited till the last minute to do his taxes.
- He hated paying fines and late charges.

So we devised a plan for organizing his tax-related papers. At first, he simply threw everything into a box, which could be tucked away in a closet or even under the bed. The contents still needed sorting and organizing at tax time, but at least all the papers were in one spot and nothing was missing or misplaced. Later, he started using a box with big, labeled envelopes as a filing system, eventually replacing it with a plastic box with hanging files, which he purchased at an office supply store. (You might want to try Eddie's habit of every so often visiting office supply stores just to see what products are available that would make your life easier or more organized.)

I also helped Eddie draw up a timetable for working on his taxes. As the papers start to accumulate months before the deadline, Eddie begins to back-time. He decides when he wants to mail the completed returns. Then he sets the date—marks it on his calendar—when he will complete the forms, and finally, the date when he needs to start working on them. Whether you go to a professional tax preparer or you handle the job yourself, you, too, can get in the habit of back timing.

As part of your planning, imagine yourself doing the work. What will you need? Certain forms or information? Advice or coaching from someone? Particular tools such as a calculator or software? Do you need to make an appointment with someone? Write this all down on your list. Deliberately set target deadlines much earlier than absolutely necessary. Then decide on small, meaningful rewards that will motivate you to accomplish various aspects of the job by the target dates, and write down a big delightful reward for when the whole job is complete, the income tax returns are in the mail, and you have your copies of everything safely filed away.

Today, Eddie, with the help of computer software, confidently does his own tax returns. All the tips and techniques he's using help him wrap up the project long before the April 15 deadline. He says the "other Eddie," who used to put off everything till the last minute, is gone forever.

THE HIGH COST OF INTEREST

One area where procrastination can have a negative impact on your finances is late fees. This includes the outrageous fees for bouncing a check. (You procrastinated about balancing your checkbook and didn't realize you needed to put funds into your account.) Occasionally missing the deadline for paying a charge card or utility bill, or for returning a library book or video, doesn't have a profound effect on your cash situation, but if you make a habit of this, you'll have to pay fines and late charges that cause your hard-earned cash to dribble away.

Add up all the late charges and fees you pay over a year's

time, and see if the total makes this an issue worth working on. Cass, who is single, mentioned to me that she had been meaning to zero out all her charge cards but there was always something she had to buy. The combined balance of her five charge cards consistently remained around $7,000 for several years. It seemed nothing could motivate her to stop making purchases with those charge cards, and she justified this habit by saying, "The interest each month really isn't that much." She had been lured into using some low-interest cards but forgot that after the initial promotional period, those interest rates skyrocketed to 17 percent and often higher. Also, some charge cards raise the interest rate if a payment is late.

When we looked at the amount of interest she paid for each card (15.5%, 17.5%, two cards at 18%, and one at 21%), the average interest that Cass paid on that $7,000 per year was 18 percent, which totaled $1,260 each year! Cass realized that the interest she was paying every year would easily cover a seven-day Caribbean cruise—something she thought was beyond her wildest dreams. She also discovered that the "few" times she paid late fees on each charge card added up to over $200 per year.

Suddenly Cass was motivated. She cut up all her charge cards except two: One charge card stayed in her dresser drawer for emergencies in case she *had* to buy something and it was not possible to save for it. Keeping it at home eliminated "impulse" buying. The other charge card, which she kept in her wallet, was for the gas station only. After almost a year, she started using a debit card, because she didn't like carrying much cash and she did not want to start using charge cards again.

She set a realistic time frame to pay off her accounts, streamline purchases, simplify her lifestyle, and be more mindful of what she was buying. In only twenty-two months, Cass was debt free and has remained debt free for several years now.

Best of all, Cass used the money that would have gone toward paying interest to take a Caribbean cruise during each of the last two winters. She truly has conquered financial procrastination and found a heavenly solution to coping with winters in the Midwest!

Small amounts of money leaking out of holes caused by procrastination can add up to large amounts over time, just as small amounts saved regularly can also add up.

BUSINESS EXPENSE STATEMENTS

Do you put off submitting expense statements for reimbursement? If so, you'll accrue interest on everything you charged, and you won't ever be reimbursed for that interest. That's one more hole for your hard-earned cash to leak through.

Start plugging the leak by identifying which part of this process is your problem. Do you wait for weeks and months, and by then you can't remember half of what should be included or what receipts you should be track-

COUPON CLIPPERS

Using coupons and rebates can save you big bucks, but only if you use them. For some people, this is one of those small but irritating areas of procrastination.

- Do you let newspapers and magazines pile up because someday you'll clip the coupons you saw?
- Do you ever go to the store with coupons, buy the items, but forget to use the coupons?
- Have you ever proudly dug out a coupon and handed it over to the checkout clerk, only to be told that your coupon expired . . . a long, long time ago?
- Do you tuck coupons all over the place (in drawers, cups, cabinets, books, wallets, etc.), where they expire without ever making it to a store?
- Have you ever bought something that had a rebate coupon, but never got around to mailing it? Or did you have the rebate coupon but couldn't redeem it because you couldn't find the receipt?

Coupons and rebates won't make you a millionaire, but procrastinating about using them makes you feel you aren't staying on top of the little things. So either decide to commit to using coupons, employing the strategies in this book to set up a system that works for you, or decide you're not going to bother with them at all, thereby eliminating the problem.

ing down? Do you need to find a place to put all your receipts and papers as they accumulate, or a system for organizing them?

Expense forms and procedures vary, even within the same occupation, so do some research. Ask others in your industry and position what they do to keep organized and to streamline the process; or ask for specific solutions, such as how they keep track of and report nonreceipt items such as tips. Write on your to-do list, "Fill out expense forms," and mark a certain time on your calendar (for example, every Friday at 10:00 A.M.) for doing this paperwork. If gathering or finding receipts is the difficulty, establish "a place for everything." It doesn't matter whether it is a file, a box, or an envelope. What matters is that you have a place to put your receipts and that you put them there.

Of course, once you have a system in place, and have established a solid habit of doing your expenses in a timely manner, don't forget to plan a reward to look forward to once the dreaded job is complete.

PLAN A SAVINGS STRATEGY

You might have a short-term savings plan for a vacation or a down payment, or a long-term plan for a college education or a comfortable retirement. Whatever your goal, the key is to decide to live below your income so there is money left to invest, and then invest it. Maybe you can

Grants, Scholarships, and Financial Aid

Procrastinating about applying for grants, scholarships, or financial aid can rob you of money and opportunities. Applications received after the deadline are usually thrown out.

You can avoid these problems through back timing. Decide when you want or need to mail the application. Then set a target deadline for going through it—making a list of what papers and information you need to gather and the people you need to write to or call.

A student I know sat down a week before the deadline to go through a financial aid application. He found out he needed transcripts from his previous school, but when he called to request them, he discovered that the request had to be made in writing. With only seven days left, he missed the deadline, lost his opportunity for financial aid, and jeopardized his chance to attend school that semester. Back timing could have prevented this disaster.

afford only a small amount to begin with, but if you save a *small* amount on a regular basis, over time it will add up. Certainly, any savings plan yields more money than no savings plan at all.

As a young boy, Michael had a paper route, and when he came home with his first paycheck, he told his mom all the things he planned to buy. She told him, "No matter how small the amount, pay yourself first." She was teaching him to develop a savings plan, then she helped him implement it. After he'd accumulated ten dollars in his plastic Superman bank, together they took all the coins and opened a savings account at their local bank. Michael's mom continued reminding him that no matter what he wanted or needed to buy, "Pay yourself first." They became a regular sight—Michael and his mom walking into the bank and stepping up to the counter, Michael handing over between five and ten dollars' worth of coins plus his savings passbook to the teller, who'd enter the amount and hand the book back to Michael. He loved seeing his money add up.

Years later, when it was time to buy his first car, Michael's savings account allowed him to buy the car he wanted. All during college he worked, and he continued to take some portion of his paycheck (no matter how small) to pay himself first. Whenever he desperately needed cash, his savings account was always there to "save" him.

In his early twenties, he and his new bride, Danielle, had enough money for a down payment on a house, primarily because of Michael's habit of saving. The couple now have two little boys, and Danielle is working a part-time job so she can be available to raise their young family. It has become harder for them to save because there never seems to be enough money to pay the bills. Even so, Michael and Danielle have set up a very small savings plan; thirty dollars is automatically withdrawn monthly from their checking account and put in a mutual fund, utilizing a concept called "dollar-cost averaging." Many of their friends don't have a savings plan because they think they can't afford to invest large amounts of money at this stage of their lives, so they save nothing. But Michael and Danielle believe that their investment of thirty dollars, or a dollar a day, is affordable even during this low-income, high-expense period. They assume that their finances will improve once the boys are in school and Danielle works full-time, and as their income increases, they intend to increase the amount they invest monthly.

Robert Jackway, a financial adviser, prepared two tables for Michael and Danielle. The first one (see table A) shows that even if they never increased the amount saved, in twenty years they would have put in $7,200; if the annual return was 10 percent, their investment would be worth $21,152. Of course, it is likely that this couple will increase their monthly investment. Robert's second table (see table B) shows that a slightly larger investment of fifty dollars each month (less than two dollars per day) at the same rate of return would in twenty years be a total investment of $12,000, which would be worth $35,254.

Robert told Michael and Danielle, "Procrastination

costs you money," and as a financial adviser, he sees examples of this every day. Let's say a couple waits five years to start saving that thirty dollars per month. All things being equal, the accumulated value at the fifteen-year mark would be $11,734 (see table A), compared to Michael and Danielle's $21,152 at the twenty-year mark. The money invested would be only $1,800 less, but the value would be almost $10,000 less. To put off for five years saving one dollar per day, at an annual return of 10 percent, would be a loss of almost $10,000. Procrastination can be expensive.

Once you decide to start a savings plan and determine the amount to regularly invest, you may discover a procedure that will make depositing money easy. Some companies allow you to direct-deposit into your savings account a portion of your paycheck. Many banks and investment plans can be set up to automatically deduct from your checking account and add to your savings account. There are many new options designed to help make the process of financial investment more convenient; you will be amazed and delighted at how small amounts of money *regularly* invested can add up for you.

Financial procrastination takes many forms. This chapter is not meant to give you financial advice. It simply shows how you can apply the principles for conquering procrastination toward gaining control over your finances and realizing your hopes and goals for financial security.

TABLE A. ACCUMULATION OF SAVINGS WITH MONTHLY DEPOSITS
OF THIRTY DOLLARS FOR TWENTY YEARS

Prepared for Michael and Danielle
Prepared by Robert C. Jackway, CLU, ChFC

Assumes monthly deposits of 30 dollars for 20 years with annual interest earned at the rate of 10 percent

End of year	Accumulated Deposits[a]	Accumulated Tax Savings (If Any)	Accumulated Earned Interest	Accumulated Value
1	360	N/A	9	369
2	720	N/A	56	776
3	1,080	N/A	142	1,222
4	1,440	N/A	274	1,714
5	1,800	N/A	455	2,255
6	2,160	N/A	689	2,849
7	2,520	N/A	984	3,504
8	2,880	N/A	1,343	4,223
9	3,240	N/A	1,775	5,015
10	3,600	N/A	2,286	5,886
11	3,960	N/A	2,884	6,844
12	4,320	N/A	3,577	7,897
13	4,680	N/A	4,376	9,056
14	5,040	N/A	5,291	10,331
15	5,400	N/A	6,334	11,734
16	5,760	N/A	7,517	13,277
17	6,120	N/A	8,854	14,974
18	6,480	N/A	10,360	16,840
19	6,840	N/A	12,054	18,894
20	7,200	N/A	13,952	21,152

[a] This amount is less sales charge, loading, or administrative costs, if any.

For ledger illustrations of a specific savings or investment plan, consult with our adviser. This is only a generic illustration.

Table B. Accumulation of Savings with Monthly Deposits of Fifty Dollars for Twenty Years

Prepared for Michael and Danielle
Prepared by Robert C. Jackway, CLU, ChFC

Assumes monthly deposits of 50 dollars for 20 years with annual interest earned at the rate of 10 percent

End of year	Accumulated Deposits [a]	Accumulated Tax Savings (If Any)	Accumulated Earned Interest	Accumulated Value
1	600	N/A	16	616
2	1,200	N/A	93	1,293
3	1,800	N/A	237	2,037
4	2,400	N/A	457	2,857
5	3,000	N/A	758	3,758
6	3,600	N/A	1,149	4,749
7	4,200	N/A	1,640	5,840
8	4,800	N/A	2,239	7,039
9	5,400	N/A	2,958	8,358
10	6,000	N/A	3,810	9,810
11	6,600	N/A	4,806	11,406
12	7,200	N/A	5,962	13,162
13	7,800	N/A	7,294	15,094
14	8,400	N/A	8,819	17,219
15	9,000	N/A	10,556	19,556
16	9,600	N/A	12,528	22,128
17	10,200	N/A	14,756	24,956
18	10,800	N/A	17,267	28,067
19	11,400	N/A	20,089	31,489
20	12,000	N/A	23,254	35,254

[a] This amount is less sales charge, loading, or administrative costs, if any.

For ledger illustrations of a specific savings or investment plan, consult with our adviser. This is only a generic illustration.

꠲

The safest way to double your money is to fold it over once and put it in your pocket.

—*Kim Hubbard*

Some debts are fun when you are
    acquiring them,
But none are fun when you set about
    retiring them.

—*Ogden Nash*

Debt is the worst poverty.

—*Thomas Fuller*

Motivation is when your dreams put on work clothes.

—*Hal Roach*

How different our lives are when we really know what is deeply important to us, and keeping that picture in mind, we manage ourselves each day to be and to do what really matters most.

—*Stephen R. Covey*

Regret for the things we DID can be tempered
   by time;
it is regret for the things we did NOT do
   that is inconsolable.

—Sydney J. Harris

A man in debt is so far a slave.

—Ralph Waldo Emerson

Never spend your money before you have it.

—Thomas Jefferson

Once you make a decision, the universe con-
spires to make it happen.

—Ralph Waldo Emerson

EXTRA CREDIT

1. Do you procrastinate about some financial matters? If so,
   what are they? _____

   _____

2. Are you happy with the amount of debt you have? Do
   you want to change it? _____

   _____

3. Are you happy with your savings plan? Do you want to change it? _____

_____

4. What financial goals do you want to achieve this year?

_____

_____

5. What are your financial goals for five years from now?

_____

_____

6. Do you need to see a financial adviser to formulate these answers?_____

_____

10

What Dreams Are Made Of

❧

WE PROCRASTINATE ABOUT a myriad of things both big and little—chores, gifts, relationships, phone calls, deadlines, joining or quitting organizations—but one of the most common (and saddest) things we put off is our dreams.

Tucked away in a secret corner of our hearts is that college degree or those music lessons or that business to start or that mountain to climb or that book to write. They are all being put off until . . . someday. When you pursue your dreams, you tap into an unlimited source of energy and enthusiasm. When you don't pursue your dreams, there is a sadness and a sense of "I wonder what would have happened if I had . . ." As John Greenleaf Whittier wrote:

> *For of all sad words*
> *of tongue or pen,*
> *The saddest are these,*
> *"It might have been."*

Barbara, who works with senior citizens, says that the majority of people who have reached the winter of their lives seldom regret the things they've done, no matter how stupid or nutty. But they do regret the things they never tried, the dreams they never followed.

So as you embark on your journey of conquering procrastination, you will find you start to achieve small successes here and there. Enjoy them. Be proud of them. Then let your successes motivate you to take a close look at how you're living. When people take stock of their lives and come up feeling empty, it's often because they have procrastinated in choosing the direction they want their lives to go. They've gotten lost in the busy-ness of day-to-day routines and put off scheduling time for fun, joy, relationships, and future goals. They've lost touch with their dreams.

What do you value? As you decide what you want your life's achievements to be, take a moment to determine what "achievement" means to *you*:

- Do you have the marriage or family or single status you wanted? That's an achievement.
- Are you working or spending leisure time in the field of your choice? That's an achievement.
- Are you raising your children to be semicivilized, almost socially acceptable human beings? Now, that's a *real* achievement.
- Have you acquired or are you working on skills you hoped to have? That's an achievement.
- Do you have friends or family that you cherish? Lucky you—that's an achievement.

- Have you survived a divorce or death of a loved one or illness or financial setback or the loss of a job, with your sanity and self-esteem intact? These are all achievements.

WHAT PATH FOR YOUR LIFE'S JOURNEY?

As we speed through life, living on the edge at a faster and faster pace, we must stop and:

- review our values
- connect with people
- decide the direction of our lives and how we want to spend our time, money, and energy
- take care of ourselves and recharge our batteries
- devise a plan
- find time for peace and quiet
- make room for love in our lives.

Noah, who attended a Conquer Procrastination seminar for college students, told the group the following story, which illustrates the importance of stopping to take stock and to determine the "path" we want to follow in life. One summer, when Noah was a wrangler at a dude ranch, he discovered an old trail in the pine forest and mentioned it to a group of riders. They were all enthusiastic and wanted to ride the trail, so Noah went ahead to make sure it was clear of fallen logs and other debris. When the group cantered across the meadow to the top of a hill, they looked down on Noah at the edge of the forest riding back and forth, searching for the trail. From their vantage point on the hill, the open spot in the trees where the trail began was obvious, but Noah was too close to it and kept riding right past.

Like Noah, many people are so breathlessly busy that they feel they have no time to stop, to plan. Those frantic times are exactly when they need to pause, catch their breath, get *some distance* so they can find their way.

When you review your list of the 101 things you've been putting off, do you notice that you have been putting off life? Have you put off time for relationships, hopes, dreams? Have you put off time for fun, relaxation, joy?

My favorite comedian, Hal Roach, often ends his performance with "Live each day as if it were your last . . . and one day you'll be right!" Is your life moving at such a fast and hectic speed that you're not enjoying it? What exactly are you hurrying toward? What are you working to achieve? When will it get better? When will you enjoy your life?

Maintenance or Enrichment?

Every to-do list you make helps you plan your actions, which in turn helps you use your time better, which, in the end, determines the path your life will follow. The items on your to-do list tend to fall into one of two categories: maintenance or enrichment.

Maintenance jobs are those that are necessary to keep your life running smoothly. Many of them must be repeated daily, weekly, or monthly: cooking, cleaning, mowing the lawn, paying bills, doing the laundry.

Enrichment activities, whether short- or long-term, are those you do by choice, not because you "should" do them. I like the word *enrichment*. You usually know if you've done something enriching because it makes your life seem— well—richer. Reading a good book. Visiting a friend. Learning to juggle. Traveling someplace for pleasure. Attending a concert or a play. Taking a class. Going to the botanic garden. Decorating the house. Most of the things you do for enrichment make you feel happy and enjoy your life more. You feel a pleasant sense of achievement and satisfaction. You feel energized.

I can practically hear you saying, "But I have so many maintenance things I should do. There's never any time for the enrichment things I want to do."

Saying "I don't have time" is simply another excuse to procrastinate. When all your time is being spent on maintenance and there is no time for enrichment, that's precisely when it's time for you to adjust your priorities and change your way of thinking and planning. In fact, the more fast-paced your life becomes with work and responsibility, the more you need to allow time for enrichment.

When you feel overwhelmed or so frazzled you can't

find the energy to do anything, that's when you need to make the time to visit a friend, ride a bike, go fishing, meditate, take a trip to the museum, or go for a walk.

How do you do it? The trick is to learn to sandwich the joyful things you *want* to do between the important things you *have* to do.

ARE YOU EXHAUSTED . . . OR BORED?

I've often met healthy people who say they are too exhausted to do anything at all. I'll ask them if it's possible that they are bored. Once when I asked this question, a woman whipped out a long list of things to do and said, "Bored! How could I be bored? I'm running around all day long."

I asked if there was anything on the list that she enjoyed doing. Her answer was no. She was swamped with jobs, chores, drudgery. She had more than enough to do, but she was bored.

If you realize that days, weeks, or months have gone by and you're not enthusiastic about anything you've done, you are probably bored. And boredom is depressing, and more exhausting than digging a ditch.

If that's the case, it's time to use the to-do list to start (or get back to) a hobby or craft or sport or a musical instrument . . . to get out in nature and breathe fresh air . . .

to meet with friends . . . to do something to enrich your life, and in the process, to re-create your energy. As Dr. Norman Vincent Peale said, "Enthusiasm creates energy."

For example, you often think that you'd like to get together with old friends or spend time with your family and those special people in your life . . . but it doesn't happen. The solution is to follow Mark Victor Hansen's advice, "Don't think it! Ink it!" Actually write down on your to-do list ways to connect with people who are important to you:

- Send note to Su Lin.
- Call Joseph.
- Set up breakfast with Laurieann.

By connecting with your priorities and acting on them, you'll be adding joy to a day previously filled with boring tasks and you'll feel energized. You can then come back to the daily chores with a new zest for life and a more loving, caring, giving attitude.

There's a time to stick to maintenance tasks and a time to put them aside. Remind yourself that when your maintenance tasks are completed, there will always be another list of more to do. But there isn't always another tomorrow for enjoying family and friends, so don't postpone sharing moments of connection or fun, relaxation or joy.

FINDING TIME TO ACHIEVE
YOUR DREAM

As you look at the maintenance and enrichment items on your list, as you prioritize, you may *still* find yourself saying, "I don't have time to achieve my dream!"

Maybe you don't. Or maybe this isn't the right time of your life to chase that dream. But maybe—just maybe—you could find some time if you decided to. Anthony Robbins, one of my favorite authors and speakers, says, "It is in the moment of decision that your destiny is shaped."

If you decide to pursue your dream, you probably will find the time to make it happen. A dream isn't the sort of thing that can be written on your "List of Things to Do Today." Dreams usually involve all kinds of different segments: investigating, learning, gathering, planning, setting up, doing. Start by answering the following questions:

1. Can I break down my dream into smaller components?
2. Do I have any available time to attend to any of these?

We discussed overwhelming jobs in chapter 6, "Help! I'm Overwhelmed." Dreams, too, are overwhelming, but when you start to make a list of all the little tasks involved, you may find that at least one task is manageable at this time in your life. Kathy, a young mother of three preschoolers, realized that she couldn't possibly become a full-time college student with all the demands of her family. So she set a goal to take just one college class each semester. By the time her youngest child started first grade,

Kathy had already completed almost two years of college.

Maybe you don't have time to learn to play the piano right now, but you could find time to shop for a piano or have yours tuned or start checking around for a good piano teacher.

Maybe you don't have time to become a writer right now, but you could find time to take a class in creative writing or word processing or marketing your writing.

Take a look at your dream. Write a list of the small steps it would take to get started. Then search for ways to find more time to make your dream a reality.

Put Your Leisure Time to Good Use

Consider how your leisure time is spent—especially your relaxing and unwinding time, and this includes sleep. Of course people need to sleep. Most doctors say the average person needs seven to eight hours sleep per night, although needs vary. How many hours do you sleep? Do you sometimes sleep not because you're tired but simply because you're bored?

How many hours are spent watching TV? If you watch TV every evening for 3½ hours, that's 24½ hours per week and 105 hours per month.

I can hear you saying: "But wait a minute. I work hard! Don't I deserve to relax sometime?" Of course you do.

I teach stress management skills in addition to skills for conquering procrastination and managing time. And in this high-stress world, relaxation is imperative for both good mental and physical health. But as you search to find available time to pursue your dream, take a good look at how much time you're spending monthly on leisure activities and ask, "Do I really need 105 hours a month to relax?"

I'm definitely not advocating that you give up all your relaxation, but when you look at the amount of time you spend unwinding, it's possible that you can find a couple of hours per week to pursue your dream.

Take Advantage of Commuting Time

Commuters who travel by bus or train may have one or two hours a day they could use constructively. Author Scott Turow, a practicing attorney with an enormously busy schedule, wrote *Presumed Innocent* and several other best-selling novels while riding the train to work. If you live thirty minutes from work, that's one hour a day of travel time or over twenty hours a month.

If you commute by car, an audiotape or CD player can be a great tool to help you pursue your dream. Use either one built into the dashboard or a portable one placed on the seat with an adapter plugged into the cigarette lighter. If you commute by bus or train, use a battery-operated player with earphones. The cost of buying twenty hours' worth of tapes or CDs per month could be outrageously expensive. The best source of free audio material is your neighborhood library. If your library doesn't carry the topics you want, you can ask the librarian to borrow them from another library.

Here are examples of how three people have used tape or CD players to turn commuter hours into useful time.

Cassidy, a corporate vice president, was planning a vacation in Germany. Six months before her trip, she bought a set of "Learn to Speak German" CDs to listen to in her car. She said she had to play each one over and over before moving on to the next one, but she had a good, basic grasp of the language by the time she left for her vacation.

Joyce, a waitress who hates her job, has started a part-time business selling products at home parties with the hope that someday it will become her full-time work. She borrows marketing, business, and motivational tapes from the library and listens on her headset as she rides the bus to her full-time job. Her home-party business is booming, and Joyce has grown to love her listening time during the long bus ride. She plans to leave her job by the end of the year and expand her part-time business into a full-time career.

Jason's dream was to buy a "handyman's special" house, fix it up, then sell it. Well, he bought the house, then procrastinated for five years before starting to fix it up. Now he listens to "positive thinking" motivational tapes during his forty-five-minute commute to and from work. He claims that this gets his juices flowing and inspires him to spend a few hours many evenings after work remodeling his house.

తango

Never curse commuting time. Simply
find a way to let it work for you.

—*Ted Schwarz,* Time Management for Writers

తango

Have you been wanting to read some of the great classics of literature or just a good popular novel? Many of them are available on tapes.

Do you want to improve your time management skills? Develop your stress management skills? Become more creative? Learn to negotiate? Listen to more music? Study selling techniques? Deepen your spirituality? Start your own business? Explore a distant culture? Many libraries have access to wonderful sets of tapes on these and dozens of other topics.

Pass It on to Others

Once you start to conquer procrastination, you can begin sharing your techniques and your successes with a friend or family member.

When my friend Julie and three of her friends rode mules down to the bottom of the Grand Canyon and back, her teenage daughter, Anna, said, "Boy, you've been talking about that dream since I was a little kid. Hmmm. Maybe someday my dreams can come true. too." Of all the gifts we can give to the children in our lives, that's a pretty great one—the belief that their dreams can come true.

Sometimes people ask my advice about how to get someone else to stop procrastinating.

If you read this book to convert some procrastinators in your life, you won't have much luck unless *they* want to change. You might have some success by explaining a few of the concepts from this book to the procrastinators. Or by encouraging them to read this book. Also, understanding why people procrastinate may give you insight that helps you deal more constructively with the procrastinators you know. But the decision to stop procrastinating must be made by the procrastinators themselves.

Create the Life You Want

Even people who are not procrastinators—those anticrastinators—have that secret letter they've been meaning to write or that secret closet that needs to be cleaned. Nobody accomplishes everything they want, but anticrastinators accomplish what's important to them.

For Katie, an executive administrator for the legal department of a major corporation, the difference between being a procrastinator or an anticrastinator comes down to a matter of control. When she used to be a procrastinator, everything seemed out of her control. She truly didn't know what she would ever get accomplished or what she wouldn't. Katie says she was afraid to volunteer for any job on any committee, because she was always scared she'd never finish what she was supposed to do. She would see a deadline looming, and her stomach would tie in knots. When she knew she had to make a tough phone call, her palms dripped with sweat.

Today, the old out-of-control feeling is gone. "The items in my life that are not accomplished are all ones I can live with," says Katie. "And the items that are really important will get done—I'll see to it by prioritizing. I may have to use every technique, every trick in the book [this book, of course], but I know I will complete whatever needs to be completed."

Like Katie you can conquer procrastination and gain a sense of control over your life. This leads to a wonderful sense of confidence. And as you become a more confident anticrastinator, you'll find yourself able to tackle larger issues, such as losing weight, quitting smoking, drug or alcohol abuse, gambling, or other negative situations in your life. Each success leads to more success; small achievements lead to bigger ones.

Granted, even when you stop being a procrastinator, you won't always be on top of things. There will be ups and downs just as in any other aspect of life. People who are working on positive thinking, or improving their spirituality, or raising their self-esteem, or whatever, all experience days when they feel they have improved enormously and reached their goals; but they also experience days of setbacks and feelings of failure.

You'll have days when you feel you don't even know the word *procrastination*, because you are so terrific at getting things done. And other days when you say, "Oh, no . . . I'm putting things off again!"

Don't panic. Don't be discouraged. If you feel yourself backsliding into a procrastination slump, here are a few ideas to get yourself back on track. Reading them might generate other ideas of your own.

- To begin with, talk out loud about your concerns. Say to someone, "You know, I've become a high-functioning, organized person, but lately I'm slipping back to my old procrastinating ways, and I hate it." Describe what it is you have been putting off, then decide what you need to do to accomplish it.
- Look back through this book to "recharge your battery." Something you've highlighted or underlined might give you the jump start you need.
- Try writing a list.
- Find a reward that might motivate you.
- Determine whether it's just the start of the job that you are dreading.

- Work on the job for an hour, setting the kitchen timer before you start.
- Write out some motivating messages, such as a sign on your refrigerator that says, "Finish the job!" or a card in your wallet that says, "Strive for Excellence, not Perfection."
- Explore any fears that might be holding you back.
- Break the job down into smaller tasks.
- Figure out a way to make the job more pleasant; try working to music or outdoors or with a friend.
- Submerge yourself in positive self-talk; explode those excuses; blow away those limitations you put on yourself.

Most of all, don't berate yourself. If you are off track, you'll get back on track. One of the biggest changes in my life now that I'm a recovering procrastinator is that I am no longer waiting for some stress to end, or a busy time to be over, or a crisis to be solved so that I can finally be happy. I've stopped putting off happiness "till later" and am loving and living life to its fullest right now. So can you.

You can change your old procrastinating ways. Don't forget Emmett's Law: The dread of doing a task uses up more time and energy than doing the task itself. So go ahead and get started creating the life you want. You deserve a great one!

I shall be telling this with a sigh
Somewhere ages and ages hence:
Two roads diverged in a wood, and I—
I took the one less traveled by,
And that has made all the difference.

—from Robert Frost, "The Road Not Taken"

The 3 great requirements for a happy life are:
something to do,
something to love,
and something to hope for.

—Joseph Addison

Some of us have great runways already built for
us, so if you have one TAKE OFF. If you don't,
grab a shovel and build one.

—Amelia Earhart

"For I know the plans I have for you," declares
    the Lord,
"Plans to prosper you and not to harm you;
Plans to give you a future and a hope."

—Jeremiah 29:11

Goals are dreams with a deadline.

—Dottie Walters

What you are is God's gift to you;
What you make of yourself
is your gift to God.

—Unknown

If one advances confidently, in the direction of his own dreams and endeavors to lead the life which he has imagined, he will meet with a success unexpected in common hours.

—*Henry David Thoreau*

You make a living by what you get, you make a life by what you give.

—*Will Rogers*

If you keep getting lost in your work, you can be pretty sure you're following the right path in life.

—*Unknown*

We're getting more done in less time but where are the rich relationships, the inner peace, the balance, the confidence that we're doing what matters and doing it well?

—*Stephen R. Covey, A. Roger Merrill, and Rebecca R. Merrill,* First Things First

EXTRA CREDIT

(two thought-provoking questions and a poem)

1. What contribution do you want to make to this world?
2. How will your having lived here leave this world a better place?

Count your nights by stars, not shadows
Count your days by smiles, not tears
And on any birthday morning
Count your age by friends, not years.

—*Unknown*

If you have thoughts or comments about this book, or would like information about other products and services offered by Rita Emmett, contact her at:

Emmett Enterprises, Inc.
2331 Eastview Drive
Des Plaines, IL 60018

Phone: 847-699-9950
Fax: 847-699-9951
Web site: www.ritaemmett.com
E-mail: remmett412@aol.com

Index

❦